The National Economy

AN INTRODUCTION TO MACROECONOMICS

Introduction to Economics Series
Kenyon A. Knopf, Editor

The National Economy

AN INTRODUCTION TO MACROECONOMICS

Gordon Philpot
WHITMAN COLLEGE

John Wiley & Sons
NEW YORK   CHICHESTER   BRISBANE   TORONTO

Library of Congress Cataloging in Publication Data:
Philpot, Gordon, 1927-
    The national economy.

    (Introduction to economics series)
    Includes indexes.
    1. Macroeconomics.   I.   Title.
HB172.5.P47   339   80-20615
ISBN 0-471-05591-3

Printed in the United States of America

10 9 8 7 6 5 4 3 2 1

To Sonja

About the Author

Gordon Philpot is an associate professor of economics at Whitman College, located in Walla Walla, Washington.

After serving in the British army, he came to the United States in 1963, attended Santa Barbara City College and the University of California at Santa Barbara, and obtained a B.A. degree in 1965. He did his graduate work at the University of Wisconsin and received a Ph.D. degree in 1969.

Dr. Philpot has written articles on British economic history and international trade theory.

Preface

Elementary Macroeconomics is designed specifically to cover the macroeconomic segment of either a one-semester or a one-year course in Principles of Economics, and to give the instructor the maximum flexibility in choice of material. To this end, chapters are divided into sections (Roman numerals) and subsections (capital letters). Depending on the instructor's preferences and the amount of time available, chapters, sections, and even subsections may be omitted without necessarily causing problems of continuity. No material is relegated to an appendix, which encourages the more eager students to read unassigned material—a highly desirable state of affairs.

Chapter 1 serves as an introductory chapter, reviews supply and demand, and explains why that microeconomic tool is unsuitable for the analysis of many macroeconomic problems. Chapter 2 introduces fundamental concepts by way of the circular flow mechanism, while Chapter 3 defines and explains some further important ideas. The consumption and saving functions are introduced in Chapter 4 and used in Chapter 5 to determine the level of national income and GNP. Each of these chapters makes use of both geometry and algebra, since experience shows that students are about evenly divided in their preferences for one or the other approach.

Chapter 6 considers the topic of fiscal policy, and the next two chapters introduce money and monetary policy. Chapter 9 ties together a variety of loose ends through the agency of $IS-LM$ analysis; again, this material may be omitted without any loss of continuity if it is felt to be too challenging. However, I feel that it is presented in an easily understandable manner and hope that students will attempt the chapter. Chapter 10 answers one of the most frequently asked questions in a beginning economics course: "How can we have both inflation and unemployment occurring together and what can be done about it?"

Chapter 11 examines, at a very simple level, some theories of economic growth and of the business cycle. Finally, Chapter 12 looks at some post-Keynesian viewpoints—alternative theories of the consumption function, monetarism, rational expectations, and the Laffer curve.

The macroeconomic component of a basic one-semester principles course might cover Chapters 1 to 4, Sections I, II, and XI of Chapter 5, Chapters 6 to 8 and Section 1 of Chapter 9. Some instructors might prefer to omit Section VIIA of Chapter 3.

When more time is available—in a one-year principles course, for example—Chapters 1 to 8 and Section I of Chapter 9 may be supplemented with further material from the last four chapters depending on the instructor's interests.

Even when time precludes a discussion of Chapter 10, I would strongly urge that students be encouraged to read it. To leave the impression that macroeconomics has nothing to say on the subject of simultaneous inflation and unemployment would be a sure way to turn off today's issue-oriented students.

Many people have contributed directly or indirectly to this work. George Lamson of Carleton College, Philip Friedman of Boston College, Dennis Johnson of the City College of San Francisco, Dennis Heffley of the University of Connecticut, and Michael Tannen made useful comments on the manuscript during its development. Kenyon Knopf, a friend and colleague, provided inspiration, guidance, and support. As all classroom teachers can appreciate, perhaps my greatest thanks should be reserved for my students at Whitman College who read and worked with the manuscript through many semesters of introductory macroeconomics.

Gordon Philpot

Introduction to Economics Series

Teachers of introductory economics seem to agree on the impracticality of presenting a comprehensive survey of economics to freshmen or sophomores. Many of them believe there is a need for some alternative that provides a solid core of principles while permitting an instructor to introduce a select set of problems and applied ideas. This series attempts to fill that need and also to give interested readers a set of self-contained books that they can absorb with interest and profit, without assistance.

By offering greater flexibility in the choice of topics for study, these books represent a more realistic and reasonable approach to teaching economics than most of the large, catchall textbooks. With separate volumes and different authors for each topic, the instructor is not as tied to a single track as in the omnibus introductory economics text.

Underlying the Introduction to Economics Series is the pedagogical premise that students should be introduced to economics by learning how economists think about economic problems. The series contains books for use with any of several other books that apply theory to events and problems of the United States and the world economy. An approach of this kind offers a good beginning to the student who intends to move on to advanced work and furnishes a clearer understanding for those whose study of economics is limited to an introductory exposure. Teachers and students alike should find the books helpful and stimulating.

Kenyon A. Knopf, Editor

Contents

1 | What Macroeconomics Is All About

Macroeconomics, one of the two major subdivisions of economics, is barely forty years old. Its birth occurred in Cambridge, England, in 1936, with the publication of John Maynard (later Lord) Keynes's *The General Theory of Employment, Interest and Money.* Prior to that time, a student taking a beginning course in economics would have found a large part of the subject matter taken up with microeconomics. As its name suggests, microeconomics deals with the small component parts of the economy; the individual as worker and consumer, the firm, the industry, and markets for specific goods and services. It answers such questions as: "Why is the price of wheat in Kansas City $3.50 a bushel?" "Why is an unskilled laborer paid $3.20 an hour in Springfield, Illinois?"

I. SUPPLY AND DEMAND

The fundamental tool of the microeconomist is a scissorslike instrument whose blades are labeled *supply* and *demand.* Both blades reflect a relationship between the price of a good or service and a quantity: the quantity supplied in the case of supply; the quantity demanded in the case of demand.

Figure 1-1a illustrates a supply curve. It shows that as the price of wheat rises farmers increase the quantity they supply. Figure 1-1b portrays a demand curve, showing in graphic form the well-known fact that the higher the price of a product, the less that is purchased.[1]

---

1. Neither curve need be a straight line; they are drawn that way for the sake of simplicity. Mathematicians will feel uncomfortable with Fig. 1-1, which puts price, the independent

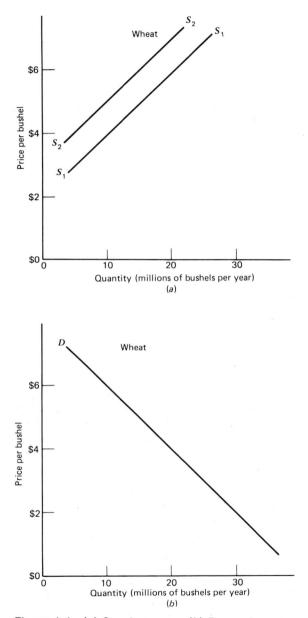

Figure 1-1. *(a)* Supply curves. *(b)* Demand curve.

Given the constraint that a sheet of paper has only two dimensions, two axes are available and are labeled *price* and *quantity* in each diagram. In the real world, of course, other variables than price affect the quantity supplied, the major one being the cost of production. Microeconomists handle this inconvenient fact very neatly by assuming that production costs remain constant for a given supply curve—labeled $S_1 S_1$ in the diagram. If production costs increase, the supply curve shifts upward, from $S_1 S_1$ to $S_2 S_2$

The most important determinants of the quantity demanded, other than the price of the product, are the consumers' incomes, the consumers' tastes, and the price of other goods. In considering the quantity of steak that consumers might purchase at a given price, for example, that quantity would increase if incomes increased, would decrease as old age reduced appetites, representing a change in tastes, and would increase if the price of pork were to rise. In constructing a demand curve, these other variables must be held constant. The Latin term for "other things held constant" is *ceteris paribus,* and this is one of the few Latin phrases to be found in the economist's vocabulary.

Another way of describing a situation when some variables are permitted to vary while others are held constant is "partial equilibrium" analysis. In a "general equilibrium" setting, by contrast, all relevant variables are permitted to vary.

The actual price of wheat is determined by the intersection of the supply and demand curves (Fig. 1-2). If the price happens to be set at $6 per bushel, producers bring 20 million bushels per year to market, only to find that consumers restrict their purchases to 10 million. In order to unload the resulting 10 million bushel surplus, producers reduce their price. Conversely, at a price of $3 per bushel, consumers would like to purchase 25 million bushels per year, but are only offered 5 million. Frustrated buyers bid up the price. Either way the price (P) gravitates toward $5 per bushel, at which price buyers and sellers are both satisfied with the quantity (Q)—15 million bushels per year.

The price of $5 per bushel and the quantity of 15 million bushels per year, as determined by the intersection of the supply and demand curves, represent an equilibrium situation. Once the price reaches $5 it tends to stay there. Furthermore, the equilibrium is stable, meaning that if the price is not at the equilibrium level it

---

variable, on the vertical axis. Alfred Marshall, the nineteenth-century British economist who pioneered the development of supply-demand analysis, drew his diagram this way and it has now become traditional.

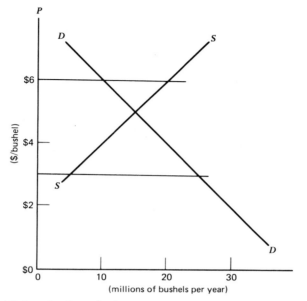

Figure 1-2. Determination of price.

gravitates toward it. An unstable equilibrium, by contrast, would be one such that if it were reached the economic forces would be in balance, but a slight shock to the system would cause a move ever further away from equilibrium.

Asking what determines price, supply or demand, is like asking which blade of the scissors cuts the paper. Both are of equal importance. This powerful tool of analysis is strictly the property of the microeconomist, but we will have occasion to refer to it in this and later chapters.

II.   THE RELEVANCE OF MACROECONOMICS

If microeconomics is concerned with the trees, macroeconomics seeks to understand the forest. It furnishes the answers to such questions as: "Why is the unemployment rate in the United States 5.8 percent?" "Why is the gross national product (GNP)[2] $2000 billion?" Three very important macroeconomic variables are listed

---

2. Many of these economic terms have by now crept into the vocabulary of the noneconomist. In any event, they will be defined formally in later chapters.

in the title of Keynes's *The General Theory.* Others would include the price level, and the inverse of employment-unemployment.

Today micro and macro stand together, of equal importance, at the core of economic theory. To be considered an economist one must master both of these major subdivisions of the discipline.

In the 1960s, the word that was always on the lips of college students was *relevance.* No subject was worthy of study, it was argued, unless it bore some relationship to the problems of the "real world," the world to be found outside the college campus, into which all students are ejected upon graduation.

The contrast between the 1960s and the 1930s is stark. A student of 1933 vintage took copious notes as a professor of economics explained that unemployment need never be a problem of any great concern, that the forces of supply and demand operating in the labor market ensure that any employer wishing to hire an extra worker can find one, that an unemployed worker seeking a job is eventually successful, and that the extra output produced by newly hired hands finds a ready market. To be sure, the professor would certainly add, such a desirable state of affairs does not prevail at all times, but any deviations from the norm are of short duration. Whenever they occur, forces are set into motion that automatically restore full employment.

That 1933 argument was based, in part, on the fallacy of composition—that what is true of the part must be true of the whole. It is true, for example, that if construction workers are unemployed because the wage in their industry is above the equilibrium level, a reduction in construction wages reduces unemployment. In Fig. 1-3, a wage rate of $7 per hour results in 200,000 construction workers being unemployed, and a reduction to $6 per hour serves to eliminate that unemployment completely. But recall the assumptions implicit in the use of such analysis. In drawing the demand curve, incomes, tastes, and the prices of other goods are assumed constant. Should any of these variables change in value, the demand curve will shift.

A reduction in the wage paid to construction workers will reduce total income somewhat, and so may affect the demand for construction workers, but if the incomes received by the 96% percent of households whose income is derived from other sources do not change, then the *ceteris paribus* assumption is not unreasonable. But when unemployment is widespread, it is indefensible to argue that a general reduction in wages, brought about by competition among the unemployed for the available jobs, reduces unemploy-

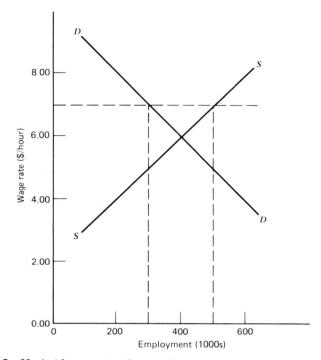

Figure 1-3. Market for construction workers.

ment. In such circumstances total income falls, and not by an insignificant amount. Finding the demand for their products turning soft, suppliers of goods and services reduce prices. In this instance the *ceteris paribus* assumption is clearly violated and the tools of microeconomics are inapplicable to the problem of large-scale unemployment.

One wonders what thoughts must have gone through the minds of those students of the 1930s. Perhaps the night before they had seen a newsreel of shabby men and women selling apples on the streets of New York. Joblessness was their plight, and the plight of millions of Americans in all parts of the country.

A student of economics could not have been unaware of the statistics. From an unemployment rate of 3 percent in 1929, the situation steadily deteriorated. Nine percent of the labor force could not find work in 1930, 16 percent in 1931, and 24 percent in 1932. In 1933, at the very depths of the Great Depression, fully one-quarter of the labor force was unemployed. It was not until 1941, with the

American economy gearing up for war, that the rate of unemployment dropped below 10 percent.[3] Clearly this was no minor deviation from a full-employment equilibrium. Even more clearly no automatic mechanism was working to ensure that equilibrium was restored.

Fortunately for the college professors of the 1930s, the demand for relevance was not to be heard for another thirty years. Even so, many of their students drew their own conclusions from the wide disparity between the classroom and the world outside. Some who joined the American Communist Party saw in the Great Depression the breakdown in the capitalist system that Karl Marx had predicted over sixty years earlier. Others became followers of Norman Thomas, believing that the solutions to the problems of their time were to be found in Socialism. But the great majority turned to the New Deal of Franklin Roosevelt, giving rise to the pattern of government involvement in economic affairs that persists to this day.

III. KEYNES AND *THE GENERAL THEORY*

When an academic discipline reaches a point when the received body of knowledge—the "conventional wisdom", to use Galbraith's phrase—becomes irrelevant to the problems of the day, a state of turmoil ensues while supporters of the old orthodoxy defend its bastions against the ever-increasing numbers of disbelievers, a turmoil that ends only when a new orthodoxy becomes accepted. *The General Theory* provided economists with a framework that seemed to fit the concerns of the 1930s—a framework that gained widespread acceptance in a relatively short period of time.

Keynes's thesis, stated briefly, was that if automatic forces do not lift the economy out of a depression, then government should intervene to restore full employment (how government might do this is discussed later). Today this view does not seem very radical, but in the 1930s, when the tenet that government governs best when it governs least still held considerable sway, it was regarded by many in much the same way that a sheep farmer views a pack of hungry coyotes. Despite Keynes's assertion that his goal was to save, not to destroy, the capitalist system, the views expressed in *The General Theory* came under strong attack. But only ten years later, its principles became the official policy of the United States government, when Congress passed, and the President signed, the Full

---

3. Source: U.S. Department of Commerce, *Historical Statistics of the United States*, 1960, p. 70.

Employment Act of 1946. In 1964, President Lyndon B. Johnson succeeded in persuading Congress to cut taxes as a means of stimulating employment. The rationale for that policy came straight from *The General Theory*. Less than ten years later, President Richard M. Nixon, a Republican where Johnson was a Democrat, was to proclaim "I am a Keynesian." At least insofar as the politicians were concerned, the acceptance of the Keynesian viewpoint seemed complete.

Yet Nixon's conversion came a little late in the day. By the 1970s, many economists were beginning to question whether the answers to the macroeconomic problems of recent years were to be found in *The General Theory*. Cynics could argue that Nixon's Keynesianism was merely a cloak under which he could hide the huge budget deficits that were a characteristic of his and, to be fair, later administrations.

IV.   MACROECONOMICS AND THE FUTURE

Once again economics is in a state of turmoil. In the 1960s economists were convinced that they had the answer to the problem of unemployment, and they thought they knew what to do about inflation. But when both came together in the 1970s, the profession found itself in disarray. George Bernard Shaw's biting criticism that if all the economists in the world were laid end to end they would never reach a conclusion appeared to have some merit. But of one thing we can be certain: the era of turmoil will be short-lived. Another Keynes will appear on the scene—he or she may even be reading these lines at this moment—and a consensus will be forged once again.

Such periods are good for an academic discipline. Without them stagnation sets in, and students turn away from a field they instinctively recognize as outmoded and irrelevant. These are exciting times in which to be studying macroeconomics.

V.   MACROECONOMICS AND GOVERNMENT
POLICY

The function of economics is not simply to explain the real world; it should be able to tell us how to change that world if we do not like it as it is. Economists have long made a distinction between these two roles. "Positive economics" seeks to explain what is; "normative economics" what should be. "Why is the unemployment rate 5.8 percent?" is a positive question. "Should the unemployment rate be

5.8 percent?" is normative. Positive economics is the meat and potatoes of the economist's meal; normative economics the icing on the cake.

These normative aspects make economics so interesting to students. When a beginning course is taught by a professor with a Ph.D. in the subject, the two-way exchange between professor and student, so vital to the learning process, would seem to be necessarily restricted. When one of the participants knows so much more than the others, one might suppose that any discussion would be rather one-sided. This statement may well be true in positive economics, where the professor's much broader experience does mean that her or his pronouncements carry more weight than those of the students. But when the discussion turns to normative matters, professor and student are on an equal footing.

Should we try to lower the unemployment rate to 5 percent? Is a 7 percent rate of inflation too high? Is the disparity between the rich and the poor too great? The Ph.D. economist will certainly have private views on these matters, and they may be strongly held, but those views are entitled to the same weight as those of any other citizen; no more and no less.

Of course, once a consensus is arrived at, the economist's expertise becomes invaluable in formulating appropriate policies to achieve the desired goal. Citizens, acting through their elected representatives, decide on society's ends; the role of the economist is to devise the means. Let us take a brief look at some of the goals that society might seek the macroeconomist's help in attaining. Any list would surely include the items shown below.

A. Full Employment

Almost everyone agrees that unemployment is undesirable. We are referring here not to the unemployment of workers who may be moving to a new location in order to better themselves, or who have voluntarily left one job in order to search for another that they think will be more satisfying. Such voluntary unemployment, often called frictional unemployment, is desirable and is a sign that the labor markets are functioning efficiently. Its existence cautions us that our goal should not be an unemployment rate of zero, but a level approximately equal to the amount of frictional unemployment, perhaps 5.5 percent in today's economy (1980), although economists disagree somewhat as to what the exact level should be.

It is involuntary unemployment that is bad. To lose one's job, and be unable to find another, degrades the spirit. Young people who are unsuccessful in obtaining employment upon graduation from high school or college become "turned off" by the system and may fritter their lives away in useless pursuits. Some families have had no means of support for three generations, apart from what they receive from welfare and other government programs.

The costs of unemployment are enormous. Not only is there an opportunity cost—the value of the goods and services that might have been produced by the unemployed—but much criminal activity may be traced directly to those who, while preferring to hold a job as the means of supporting their families, are not averse to turning to petty theft and similar crimes if that job is denied them. This is not to argue that with full employment all crime ceases, but rather to suggest that Satan does find work for some idle hands.

The incidence of mental illness and divorce always rises in time of high unemployment. This is bad in itself, but it also represents an economic loss. It is clearly a waste of resources to pay a psychiatrist $50 an hour to treat a severe depression, brought on by the loss of a job. What is needed is not therapy, but another job, to make the worker feel like a worthwhile member of society once again. The elimination of involuntary unemployment is, and should be, one of our top national priorities.

B. Price Stability

In any dynamic economy we should expect prices to be continually changing. As the demand for beef increases, its price rises; when the demand for lettuce falls, so does its price. Technological change may lead to more efficient ways of producing goods, resulting in lower prices, while natural resource prices rise as their supply is depleted. The price system serves as an extremely efficient signaling device, alerting producers and consumers alike to the need to change their habits. Such price changes are desirable, and are properly the concern of the microeconomist.

With some prices rising and some falling, the average price level need not change. But sometimes we find more prices rising than falling, resulting in an increase in the average price level, and this state of affairs may persist for some time. When it does, we are in an era of inflation. Students of college age have never experienced anything else and regard it as a fact of everyday life. Their grandparents, however, still remember the Great Depression, an era of deflation. Then average prices fell, and brought ruin to untold numbers of people in large and small businesses. Inflation and deflation concern the macroeconomist. Both are undesirable, unless kept within fairly limited bounds.

C. Economic Growth

From the dawn of history until the 1960s there was almost universal agreement that economic growth was good. More, it was believed, was better than less. Today, at least in the United States, and to a lesser degree in some of the other developed countries, voices are heard espousing the opposite view: that economic growth, because of its adverse effects on the environment—air and water pollution, the depletion of natural resources, urban blight, etc.—should no longer be a major economic goal. These voices belong to a relatively small minority, but they are becoming louder as time goes by. Is it possible that they will one day become a majority, so that the role of the macroeconomist in a democratic society will be to advise on the best methods of restraining growth?

The answer, at least for the moment, is no. Humans are extremely complicated animals, and there is much that we do not know about human behavior, but one characteristic is common to almost all Americans in the labor force. Each year they expect a wage increase sufficient to offset the effects of inflation and then a little more. In other words, they expect their real income—their standard of living—to improve over time. There is also a general expectation that each generation will be better off than its predecessor. Many parents are willing to make all kinds of sacrifices to that end—that their children might enjoy a better life than they did.

Consider what a no-growth economy would imply. On the day students graduate from college and enter the labor force, they would receive an annual salary that could never increase over an entire lifetime, unless the price level rose in proportion. Their real income could not increase.[4]

One exception to this rule is worth noting. An increase in one person's standard of living may be consistent with zero economic growth, provided that it is achieved at someone else's expense. You can have your increase of $2000 per year as long as another salary is cut by a like amount.

Therein lies the flaw in the argument against economic growth. A no-growth policy sets one group in society against another. Americans would soon resemble a pair of alley cats tied up in a sack.

---

4. The argument here is somewhat simplified. We should be comparing lifetime, not annual, incomes. Almost everyone would receive higher pay as they became more expert in the job and hence more valuable to an employer. To counteract this, as population grows, zero economic growth implies a falling standard of living as a constant level of output is shared among greater and greater numbers. To the extent that these two factors cancel each other out, the argument is valid; to the extent that they do not, it is only approximately correct.

Fortunately the choice between economic growth and a clean environment is not an either/or proposition. We can have both. But while the means to a clean environment—taxes on, and subsidies to, specific firms and industries—is the concern of the microeconomist, economic growth does lie within the purview of the macroeconomist.

D. An Equitable Distribution of Income

All economies have to find the answer to three questions: What will be produced? How will it be produced? For whom will it be produced? The great strength of a competitive free-market economy is that it answers the first two questions very well, producing the right quantity of goods and services in the most efficient manner possible. It can be argued that its response to the third question is not so good. The ability to purchase goods and services depends on one's income, which, in turn, depends on the ownership of the factors of production: labor, land, and capital.

At this point a word of warning is in order. All of the goals we are discussing lie in the realm of normative economics and involve value judgments. This statement is particularly true when applied to the question of income distribution. It is indeed perfectly legitimate to argue that the pattern of income distribution resulting from the existing scheme of factor ownership is appropriate and that one should not tamper with it.

It is equally legitimate to argue that there is nothing sacrosanct about income distribution and that it should be changed in the interests of greater equality. The existing distribution might be all right if it resulted from differences in ability, or in the will to work, but it does so only in part. The children of the rich have tremendous advantages over those whose parents are less well situated financially. Redistribution of income is necessary, the argument continues, to compensate for the unequal positions from which we embark on our economic voyages through life.

If this view is accepted, and most of us seem to think it has some validity, then the goal of attaining greater income equality may be achieved through the use of appropriate macroeconomic policies.

E. International Considerations

The means to achieve equilibrium in a country's balance of international payments under a regime of fixed exchange rates properly belongs in a book on international economics. It is briefly mentioned here, however, since macroeconomic policies can be used to influence both the pattern of trade, particularly the level of imports, and international capital movements. This particular goal has become of lesser importance since 1971, when the current system of floating exchange rates was inaugurated. Even today, however, the strength or weakness of the dollar vis à vis other currencies is affected by American domestic macroeconomic policies.[5]

VI.   MACROECONOMIC GOALS: A SYNTHESIS

Some readers may have been puzzled by the use of the term *value judgments*. Surely, they will argue, full employment is to be preferred to unemployment, price stability to either inflation or deflation, and equilibrium in the balance of payments is superior to disequilibrium. On the issues of growth and equality there is more disagreement, but even so, most of us are in favor of growth—always supposing that it can be achieved with due regard for the environment—and greater equality of incomes. Why are value judgments involved? Why not agree on our macroeconomic goals and then set about the process of learning how to achieve them?

It is not quite that simple. The problem is that policies that facilitate the achievement of one goal may be inimical to another. In some cases, it is true, we can have our cake and eat it too. A balance of payments deficit, resulting from domestic inflation, will be cured by policies designed to end inflation. Some employment stimulating policies may speed up the rate of economic growth. But policies designed to reduce income inequality will have disincentive effects that slow down the rate of growth. Antiinflationary policies can increase unemployment. Stimulating growth will almost certainly turn a healthy balance of payments account into one with an unacceptable deficit. Value judgments are involved in deciding how much progress toward one goal should be given up in order to achieve another. Were it possible to achieve all of our goals simultaneously, much of the exciting debate that goes on over economic affairs would be redundant.

VII.   SUMMARY AND CONCLUSION

The tools of microeconomics, particularly supply and demand analysis with its assumptions about "other things held constant," are unsatisfactory when it comes to analyzing the aggregate economy, in which many variables are interrelated, so that if one changes, others do too.

---

5. In 1979 the weakness of the dollar was very much on the minds of macroeconomic policymakers.

In *The General Theory,* John Maynard Keynes developed a new scheme of analysis that seemed to explain the real world of the 1930s better than the theories it was intended to replace.

The goals of macroeconomic policy include full employment, price stability, economic growth, and a more equal distribution of income. Some of these goals are mutually exclusive, and the choice between them involves value judgments. Whenever value judgments are at issue we enter the realm of "normative" economics; when attempting to describe "what is" rather than "what should be," we go into the field of "positive" economics.

QUESTIONS

1. Fig. 1-4 shows the market for shoes in the Soviet Union. An economic commissar is trying to decide between three prices for shoes: 15, 25, or 35 rubles per pair.
   (a) Which price will result in a smoothly functioning market for shoes?
   (b) Which would be most likely to result in long lines outside of shoe stores when a new shipment is expected?
   (c) Which would most likely result in shoe stores bulging with unsold merchandise?
   (d) Which price is the equilibrium price?

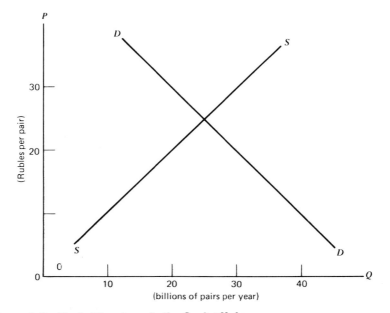

Figure 1-4. Market for shoes in the Soviet Union.

2. Which of the following is not a concern of the macroeconomist?
    (a) The rate of unemployment.
    (b) Cleaning the environment.
    (c) The rate of inflation.
    (d) The rate of economic growth.
3. Can you think of one of the few Latin phrases in the economist's vocabulary? What does it mean?

2 | A Complex Economy Simplified: (1) The Circular-Flow Approach

The American economy is an extremely complex phenomenon. In 1978 it produced goods and services with a total value of $2106 billion.[1] The dollar values of towtrucks and turnips, corn and cantaloupes, and the services of taxidermists and taxidrivers and barbers and beauticians are all included in this overall figure. To enable us to comprehend this complicated mechanism, we begin with a gross oversimplification of reality, and then, from that easily understood but distorted picture, we move one step at a time until we have achieved a reasonable compromise between simplicity and reality, which can then serve as a vehicle for further analysis.

I.   THE CIRCULAR FLOW

The starting point is the circular flow mechanism, depicted in Fig. 2-1, which illustrates the interaction between a business sector and a household sector. Business provides households with goods and services, receiving in return the factors of production it needs to produce them: capital, labor, and land.

Here another word of warning is in order. Unlike the physical scientists, who chose to use words of Greek or Latin origin, economists (*ceteris paribus* aside) have made use of the English language for their technical terms. When a chemist uses the word *sodium*, one thinks of grayish white metal that must be kept in a jar of some inert liquid, because when it comes into contact with water a chemical reaction occurs. The word *sodium* has no other meaning.

---

1. Source: *Economic Report of the President*, 1979, p. 183.

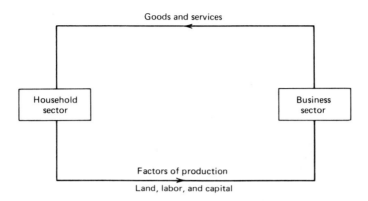

Figure 2-1. Circular flow: (1) goods and services.

The situation is not so in economics. The student must be on guard, therefore, against ascribing the everyday meaning to a word the economist is using in a strictly technical sense. One such word is *capital*. To noneconomists, it connotes money and perhaps other forms of wealth. When used in an economic context, however, *capital* refers to a factor of production that is itself produced, as distinct from labor and land, which are not. Factories, machines, and transportation equipment used to produce goods and services represent capital. They are indeed a form of wealth, but wealth of a very specific kind.

Labor to the economist has a meaning that closely parallels that of everyday life. Labor is the human factor of production. Unlike the other two, it cannot be owned—it is not a form of property—except of course in societies that permit the institution of slavery.

Land has a broader meaning to the economist than it does to the noneconomist. It does encompass agricultural land, and land on which factories may be built, but it also includes any natural resource—a deposit of copper ore, for example, or a swift-flowing river that may be used to generate electricity.

Capital, labor, and land may all be used in varying combinations to produce goods and services. They are all factors of production.

In the opposite direction to the counterclockwise flow of goods, services, and the factors of production is a flow of the dollars given and received in payment for them. We will concentrate on this clockwise money flow. It consists of a single entity—money—that can be measured in a single unit of account—the dollar. The money flow is depicted in Fig. 2-2. At the top of the diagram, the payments made by the household sector to the business sector for the goods

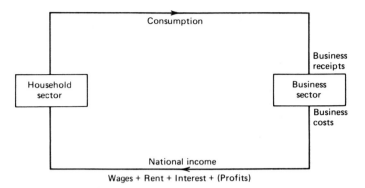

Figure 2-2. Circular flow: (2) money.

and services received, largely representing expenditures on consumer goods, is called consumption (C).

Defined formally, consumption is the total expenditure by the household sector in a given time period, almost always one year, on ·final goods and services. In this context, in this simplified version of reality, the word *final* refers to goods that are intended for sale to the consumer; in contrast to intermediate goods, which are not. By way of illustration, a new refrigerator and a new dishwasher, when sold to a household, are final goods. The electric motors that power those machines, perhaps produced for the appliance manufacturer by a subcontractor, are intermediate goods. The ball-bearing assembly, lying in a bin in a warehouse, and the machined casting, awaiting installation in an automobile engine, are intermediate goods.

The total dollar value of all the final goods and services produced in a given year is known as the gross national product (GNP). In our simplified version of reality, only consumer goods are produced, hence:

$$GNP = C$$

At the bottom of Fig. 2-2 are the payments made by business for the use of the factors of production: interest for the use of capital, wages for labor, and rent for land. The sum of these payments is known as the national income (NI).

It would be convenient if the dollar flow at the top of Fig. 2-2 were the same as the dollar flow at the bottom. That this is not so is readily seen by looking at the business sector on the right-hand side of the diagram. The flow in at the top exceeds the flow out at the bottom by an amount equal to total profits of the business sector.

This follows from the identity

$$\text{Profits} = \text{Receipts} - \text{Costs}$$

The two flows can be made equal, however, if we define national income, as we can, to include profits. We now have the following relationships:

$$NI = \text{Wages} + \text{Rent} + \text{Interest} + \text{Profits}$$
$$GNP = NI$$

Even at this very elementary stage of our analysis we can obtain some important insights into the way the economy operates. For over 100 years prior to 1936, economists believed that any good that might be produced would find a buyer. The proposition was first formulated by the French economist Jean Baptiste Say, and economists were so certain that it was true that they accorded the proposition the status of a law, a much stronger appellation than a mere hypothesis or theory. Very simply, Say's law states that supply creates its own demand. Its validity depends on the equality of the top and bottom dollar flows. The production of any good or service generates just sufficient income to pay for that good or service. Hence there cannot be a glut—goods produced that remain unsold. One of Keynes's major insights was that under certain circumstances Say's law is invalid. The business sector might produce goods and be unable to sell them.[2]

II. CALCULATING GNP: THE VALUE-ADDED APPROACH

It is one thing to define GNP; quite another to calculate it with any degree of accuracy. At first sight it seems simple enough, although time consuming, to add up the values of the goods produced by different firms. But there is more to it than that. Imagine an economy in which farmers produce wheat, millers turn the wheat into flour, bakers turn the flour into bread, and shopkeepers sell the

---

2. Actually Malthus anticipated Keynes by over 100 years, as Keynes himself admitted. Malthus knew that a glut could occur, but had difficulty in explaining how. Students who might want to reason for themselves the circumstances under which Say's law is invalid are warned that they will be unable to do so until a greater degree of complexity is introduced into the analysis.

bread to the final consumer. Suppose that the values of the goods produced are those shown in Table 2-1.

Table 2-1   Calculating GNP: An Incorrect Approach

Farmers produce	$3 million worth of wheat
Millers produce	$7 million worth of flour
Bakers produce	$12 million worth of bread
Shopkeepers sell	$15 million worth of bread
GNP	$37 million

Were we to simply examine the accounts of all of the individual farmers, millers, bakers, and shopkeepers and add the total value of all the goods they produce, we would arrive at a figure for GNP of $37 million. This figure is much too high, and involves double, triple, and even quadruple counting.

To arrive at a correct value for GNP we need to calculate the value added at each stage of the manufacturing process. Let us make the simplifying assumption that farmers start from scratch and produce $3 million worth of wheat. Millers take that $3 million worth of wheat and turn it into $7 million worth of floor. They add $4 million to its value; value added equals $4 million. By performing similar calculations for the bakers and the shopkeepers, we come up with the figures in Table 2-2.

Table 2-2   Calculating GNP: The Correct Method

		VALUE ADDED
Farmers		$3 million
Millers	7−3=	$4 million
Bakers	12−7=	$5 million
Shopkeepers	15−12=	$3 million
GNP		$15 million

Value added actually represents the payments made for the factors of production—wages, rent, interest, and profits—and thus the calculation confirms the equality of GNP and NI.

By expressing the figures in Table 2-1 as the sum of the values added, we can show how the error of multiple counting crept in.

3	+ (3 + 4)	+ (3 + 4 + 5)	+ (3 + 4 + 5 + 3) =
Farmers	Millers	Bakers	Shopkeepers
(3 + 3+ 3+ 3)	+ (4 + 4 + 4)	+ (5 + 5)	+ 3
Value added by farmers counted four times	Value added by millers counted three times	Value added by bakers counted twice	Value added by shop-keepers counted once

$$= 37 \text{ million dollars}$$

While the use of the value-added approach does give us the right answer, the thoughtful student may observe a simpler way of arriving at the correct GNP figure. The $15 million obtained by summing the values added at each stage of the production process is exactly the same as the value of the bread sold by the shopkeepers, the final link in the production chain. The wheat, flour, and bread produced by the bakers are all intermediate goods, which we know must not be included in the calculation of consumption. Why use a complex method when a seemingly much simpler approach is available?

The answer is that it will not work in the more complex world in which we live. The assumption implicit in the economy we have just examined is that all wheat is turned into flour, all flour is baked into bread, and all bread is sent to the shopkeeper. In the real world this is not so. While most of the wheat is processed and converted into other forms of food—bread, pork, spaghetti, noodles, macaroni, and so on—some is sold directly to the final consumer, perhaps in the form of pet food. Similarly, while much of the flour that the millers produce is used in the production of bread, cakes, pastry, and pies, some does end up in the hands of the final consumer, as when people purchase 10-pound bags of flour from the supermarket shelf. For this reason, the complicated value-added approach to the calculation of GNP is unavoidable.

III.   SAVINGS AND INVESTMENT

The next step we must take to bring our analysis closer to reality is to recognize that households do not spend all of their income. They also save. And not all of the output of goods and services goes to the household sector. Capital is a produced factor of production, and the business sector purchases the plant and equipment it needs to produce the goods and services it sells to the household sector.[3] These additions to the stock of capital are known as investment. *Investment* is another word that has a different meaning in an economic context than it does in everyday life. To the layperson it connotes the purchase of stocks and bonds with a view to obtaining dividends, interest, and/or capital gains. To the economist, however, it means the addition to the stock of capital that occurs in a one-year period.

Saving, the portion of income that is not spent, may be thought of as a leakage from the circular flow of Fig. 2-2. Perhaps here is the reason for the invalidity of Say's law—that the production of a good or service generates just sufficient income to ensure that it will be purchased. If some income is not spent, but saved, then some goods may indeed remain unsold, and a glut is possible.

"Not so," the pre-Keynesians—Keynes himself called them the "classical economists"—would reply. For just as saving represents a leakage from the circular flow, so investment represents an injection that, they would argue further, exactly offsets the leakage caused by saving. To see why, we need to add a third sector to our circular flow diagram: a financial sector, consisting of the nation's banks, savings and loan institutions, pension funds, insurance companies, and so on. The financial sector takes the saving of the household sector and channels it to the business sector to finance investment. The circular flow diagram, so amended, is depicted in Fig. 2-3.

That diagram also reflects one further refinement we have not yet discussed. Some investment is financed by the business sector itself. The part of business profits that is not paid out in the form of dividends to stockholders is retained within the business and may be used to finance business expansion; in a word, investment. These retained earnings, as they are called, represent a form of business saving.

The classical economists believed that the leakage caused by saving was exactly offset by the injection of investment. The mechanism whereby this equality is brought about is shown in Fig. 2-4. Saving represents a supply of loanable funds, and the classical assumption was that higher interest rates induce the household sector to save more, while lower interest rates discourage saving;

---

3. There is no inconsistency here with our assumption that the factors of production are owned by the household sector. Even when investment is undertaken by business, the household sector owns the plant and equipment that are purchased, even if that ownership is indirect, as, for example, when a member of the household sector owns shares in a corporate component of the business sector.

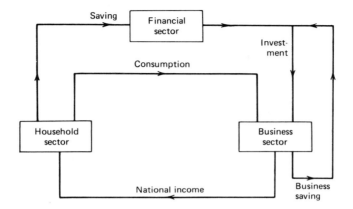

Figure 2-3. Circular flow: (3) with the addition of a financial sector.

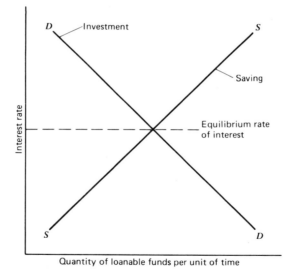

Quantity of loanable funds per unit of time

Figure 2-4. Mechanism bringing about the equality of saving and investment.

hence the usual supply curve, sloping upward to the right. By contrast, high interest rates choke off investment, which represents a demand for loanable funds; low interest rates stimulate that demand. If saving and investment are not equal, the interest rate adjusts until they are. One of Keynes's major insights was that, under certain circumstances, it might not be possible for the interest rate to fulfill the role assigned to it by the classical economists. We will discuss this topic in more detail in Chapter 8.

What are the consequences if saving and investment are not equal? If saving exceeds investment—in terms of our circular flow diagram, if the leakage exceeds the injection—the flow diminishes. The output of goods and services may decline to a level at which some of the factors of production are unemployed. If one of these unemployed factors is labor, the economy experiences unemployment in the everyday use of that term. Conversely, if investment exceeds saving—if the injection is greater than the leakage—the flow increases. With unemployed resources available they may be put to work with a resulting increase in real output. But once the economy reaches the full-employment level, no further increase in real output is possible. An increase in the dollar value of the circular flow can come about only as a result of an increase in the price level, and that is inflation.

As a consequence of these speedups or slowdowns in the circular flow, Keynes believed that a new equilibrium would be reached, with the dollar value of the circular flow constant once again, but, and this is one of the crucial elements in the Keynesian theory, there is no reason, except pure coincidence, why the volume of the flow should be at such a level that all resources are fully employed. In particular, and Keynes was, after all, a man of his time, the equilibrium level of GNP could be below the full-employment level.

Not even a general wage cut, as we saw in Chapter 1 would stimulate employment. While a wage cut would reduce business costs, enabling that sector to reduce its prices, the bottom half of the circular flow diagram would also be affected, since wages make up the major portion of national income. Keynes believed that the reduction in the price level would be offset by a corresponding decline in purchasing power.

What then can be done to stimulate employment when the economy is caught in a below full-employment equilibrium? The Keynesian analysis would seem to have the answer right away. If the circular flow is too small, its volume might be pumped up by increasing the injection, or decreasing the leakage. In other words, stimulate investment and discourage saving.

It is true that investment might be encouraged by appropriate tax policies, by giving tax breaks to companies that undertake new investment, for example. And savings may be reduced by encouraging consumption, perhaps by reducing sales taxes. But in the depths of a deep depression, businesspeople may be so discouraged that they do not want to consider plant expansion no matter what tax breaks may be available. When you cannot sell the goods you are already producing, the last thing you think of is how to increase that production. And sales taxes are one of the major means by which state governments finance their expenditures. But in any event we are getting ahead of ourselves. As soon as we discuss taxes, we are implicitly assuming the existence of a government sector, the only sector capable of levying such taxes. Let us now introduce that sector more formally into our analysis.

IV. THE GOVERNMENT SECTOR

The household sector not only consumes and saves. A portion of its income is taken in taxes. Taxes represent an additional leakage to the circular flow. The government sector, besides collecting taxes from households, makes payments to business for such items as highway construction, armaments, consulting and research services, and so on. In addition it makes payments to the household sector in the form of unemployment compensation and welfare payments. Since these payments may be envisaged as taking money from one pocket of the household sector and putting it in another, they are known as transfer payments. All of these additional flows are shown in Fig. 2-5. The business sector also pays taxes—corporate

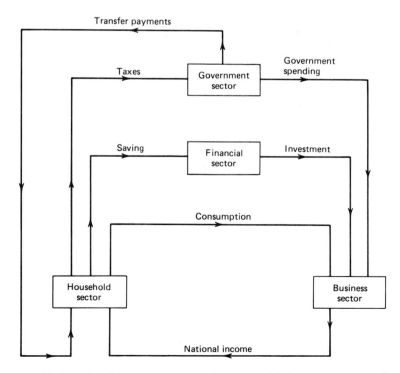

Figure 2-5. Circular flow: (4) government sector added.

income taxes, business property taxes, etc.—but in the interests of simplicity the diagram does not show them. Also in the interests of simplicity, business saving, shown in Fig. 2-3, is omitted.

The important thing about the introduction of a government sector is that it incorporates an additional leakage (taxes) and an additional injection (government spending) both of which are much more amenable to manipulation by government than are saving and investment. Government has direct control over the level of both taxation and government spending. If it desires to increase the volume of the circular flow, it may do so by increasing government spending, cutting taxes, or both. Conversely, to decrease the flow volume, the appropriate measures are an increase in taxes, a cut in spending, or both. The manipulation of taxes and spending by government to regulate the pace of economic activity is known as fiscal policy, a topic that we will take up in more detail in Chapter 6.

V.   THE FOREIGN SECTOR

For the sake of completeness, we need to add one more sector to our circular flow diagram, a sector that brings with it one more leakage and one more injection (Fig. 2-6). The need for that additional sector

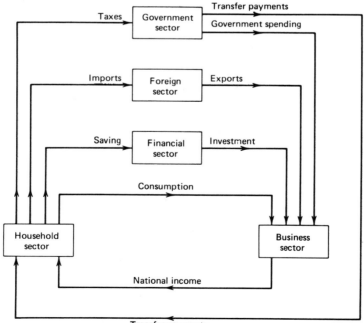

Figure 2-6. Circular flow: (5) foreign sector added.

is based on the fact that the United States does not exist in isolation. It interacts with other countries, one such form of interaction being international trade. We can think of the rest of the world as a foreign sector to which we send money (a leakage) to pay for our imports, and from which we receive money (an injection) in payment for our exports. Until fairly recently the United States did not need to concern itself overmuch with repercussions from the foreign sector. Today that situation has changed and government officials must always keep one eye on possible international ramifications when formulating macroeconomic policy.

Some countries, most notably West Germany and Japan, rely heavily on exports as a spur to economic growth. By the same token, in times of inflation the encouragement of imports not only increases a leakage from the circular flow, reducing the economic pressure, but it also enhances competition, leading to a further slowing in the rate of inflation.

VI. SUMMARY AND CONCLUSION

The circular-flow mechanism serves to introduce in an informal manner some very important macroeconomic concepts.

Say's law—the statement that supply creates its own demand— follows directly from the equality of the top and bottom flows, or, what amounts to the same thing, to the equality of GNP and NI.

GNP is calculated by summing the values added by all the firms in the economy. To simply add the values of each firm's output results in multiple counting.

In the more complex model, three leakages—saving, taxes, and imports—were introduced, together with three corresponding injections—investment, government spending, and exports. Taxes and government spending are two variables under the control of policymakers, and their manipulation to speed up, or slow down, the circular flow is known as fiscal policy.

QUESTIONS

1. If National Income is defined—as in fact it is not—as interest + wages + rents, what is the relationship between GNP and NI? Why?
2. On the planet Fosdine, which is inhabited by humanoid termites, in the Fosdinian year 20,646, foresters grew trees worth 5 Fosdinian Crukes (FCs), loggers produced logs worth 11 FCs, sawyers produced lumber worth 32 FCs, and timber merchants cut up the lumber into bite-size chunks which they then sold to the populace for 40 FCs. All trees produced went to the loggers, all logs to the sawyers, and all lumber went to the timber merchants. Calculate the Fosdinian GNP for 20,646 using the value-added approach. How can you check your answer?

3 | A Complex Economy Simplified: (2) A Further Look at Some Important Economic Variables

The circular-flow analysis of the preceding chapter introduced some very important macroeconomic concepts in an informal manner, in much the same way that an architect gets ideas to what a new building will look like by means of rough sketches. Just as the architect must proceed from rough sketches to carefully scaled drawings, so must we introduce more rigor into our analysis before proceeding further. Let us look again, therefore, at some of the concepts introduced in the last chapter, define them more carefully, and examine the interrelationships between them in more detail.

I. CONSUMPTION

As calculated in the national income accounts, consumption is more than the sum total of all expenditures by the household sector on final goods and services. The purchase of dining-room furniture is a consumption expenditure, as is money spent on holidays by the sea, magazine subscriptions, and fireworks on the Fourth of July. But sometimes a household receives a good or service for which no money payment is made, and the transaction does not show up in its accounts. Because it is regarded as being economically important, however, an estimate is made of its value—an imputed value, hence the word *imputation* is used—and the sum of such estimates is included in the total figure for consumption. Some of the more important imputations are discussed below.

A. Goods Produced and Consumed on the Farm

Most goods produced on United States farms are sold in the marketplace, either to food processors or to the household sector. But a farmer may kill a pig for home use or may supply the family's needs for dairy products and eggs. An estimate is made of the value of all these farm products and is included in the figure for consumption.

B. The Value of a Free Checking Account

Many banks provide free checking accounts for those customers who keep some minimum balance in their account. An estimated value for all such services is included in the figure for consumption.

C. The Rental Value of an Owner-Occupied Home

An apartment dweller's rent represents a payment for a service: that of being provided with a place in which to live. A person living in a private house, by contrast, while being provided with a similar service, pays no rent. An estimate is made by noting what rent is paid for rental homes of similar quality in the same neighborhood, and the sum of such estimates is included in the figure for consumption. Note that the sale of a new house enters into the national income accounts as investment, not consumption. (Investment encompasses all new structures, not excepting home construction.) The sale of a secondhand house is, of course, not reflected at all, since it does not represent current production, although the value of the services provided by a realtor or lawyer to facilitate the sale is.

II. SOME ITEMS OF ECONOMIC SIGNIFICANCE THAT ARE NOT REGARDED AS CONSUMPTION

In addition to the imputations mentioned above, it might be argued that the value of other goods and services, including some for which a cash transaction occurs, should also be treated as consumption, but in fact they are not. Some of the more important examples are listed below.

A. The Services of a Homemaker

A loaf of bread purchased at the supermarket is clearly a consumption expenditure. Should not the value of a similar loaf, baked at home by a homemaker, also be included? More generally, should not the value of all the services provided by homemakers be estimated and included in the overall figure? The answer is no, for the practical reason that the difficulty of making such an estimate is astronomi-cal.

The omission of the services of homemakers from national ac-counts can lead to problems. In 1976 GNP per capita in the United States was $7,867; in India $137.[1] Does this mean that the average American enjoys a standard of living 47 times that of the average Indian? The answer is no, for a variety of reasons that do not concern us here.[2] One reason that does is that in India a much higher propor-tion of total output is produced by the homemaker than is the case in the United States. The American homemaker who bakes bread is an exception; most pick up their loaves at the supermarket as a matter of routine. In India, most of the women in the villages bake their own bread, grind their own flour, spin the thread they weave into cloth, sew their family's clothing, and engage in many other activities that their American counterparts leave to the business sector. In comparison to the United States, therefore, India's GNP is understated because this quantitatively large amount of output is not accounted for.

B. The Fruits of Illegal Activities

The purchase of a pack of cigarettes is consumption. What about the purchase of a daily ration of heroin by a drug addict? Is that not consumption also? Again the answer is no, not because of the diffi-culty of estimating the total value of economic activities that by their very nature are not recorded in any formal manner, but instead because a line must be drawn between what is regarded as econom-ically desirable activity and what is not.

Is the killer who, for a $5000 fee, murders a judge with a record of passing harsh sentences on criminals performing an economically useful service? We recoil in horror at the question even being raised. But what about the street-corner bookie? Does the bookie not pro-vide a useful service to gamblers without the means to place their bets at the legal tote windows at the racetrack? Here the issue is less clear, and the national income accountant hates to become involved

---

1. Sources: *Economic Report of the President, 1976,* pp. 187 and 217; *Foreign Economic Trends and their Implications for the United States: India,* May 1977, U. S. Department of Com-merce.
2. The major problem is that the GNPs of the two countries are measured in different units of account, the dollar and the rupee, and so the question arises as to what is the appropriate exchange rate to use to make them directly comparable. Even when exchange rates are not distorted by government intervention, they reflect only the prices of traded goods. A haircut in India costs less than one-tenth of the cost of the same service in the United States, but this does not affect the dollar-rupee exchange rate, whereas the price of gasoline, which is roughly the same in each country, net of taxes, does.

in moral questions of this nature. The solution is the very simple one of defining economic activity as those actions that have been judged by the people as a whole, acting through their elected representatives, as worthwhile. In short, if an action is illegal it is not reflected in the national income accounts.

This eminently sensible solution does cause some minor problems. In comparing consumption in the United States for 1929 and 1979, one must recognize that while the latter figure includes the output of the liquor industry, the former does not. During the Prohibition era, which encompassed 1929, liquor, while consumed in large quantities, was consumed illegally.

Again, in comparing consumption expenditures in 1979 for the United States and Great Britain, the former figure does not include most expenditures on (largely illegal) gambling, while the latter, reflecting the fact that almost all forms of gambling are now legal in the British Isles, does. Most expenditures on abortion today show up in the national income accounts; ten years ago they did not. Once again the national income accountant avoids the moral implications. Now that abortion is legal, expenditures on it are part of consumption; when it was illegal, they were not.

III. INVESTMENT

Investment represents an addition to the nation's stock of capital. Formally, it is made up of expenditures on new structures, new producers' durable equipment, and net additions to inventories. New structures include all construction, not excepting new homes and apartment blocks, but excludes such expenditures by government. Producers' durable equipment encompasses new machinery—tractors, drills, lathes, milling machines, and so on. A good that is produced, but not yet sold, goods in the course of production—the automobile halfway along the assembly line is a good example—and raw materials awaiting processing, are all included in inventories. Net additions to inventories are a component of investment, as discussed in later analysis, and represent an exception to the general rule that only final goods and services are counted in the computation of GNP. Net reductions have a negative sign; they reduce the overall figure for investment.

Suppose that the capital stock was equal to $2000 billion on January 1, 1979, and that during that year the business sector spent $200 billion on investment projects. Does this mean that on January 1, 1980, the capital stock has increased to $2200 billion?

A moment's reflection indicates that the answer must be no. While new factories are being completed and new machinery installed, old factories and machinery are wearing out and becoming obsolete. A correction must therefore be made to the value of the capital stock to reflect this fact.

People in business do not wait until a factory literally collapses or a machine is finally transported to the scrapyard, before writing it off. A firm's accountants take a different approach. If the life of a machine is known to be ten years on the average, its value is written down each year by one-tenth of its cost, so that by the end of the tenth year its value, at least insofar as the firm's books are concerned, is zero.[3]

The accountant's—and the economist's—term for this reduction in the value of an asset at the end of the year is *depreciation*. Each year the national income accountants add up the depreciation figures for all business enterprises in the country. This sum is then subtracted from the value of the capital stock to arrive at the correct figure. Suppose that, in the example we were looking at earlier, depreciation amounted to $120 billion. The true value for the capital stock on January 1, 1980 would therefore be

$2000 billion + $200 billion − $120 billion = $2080 billion

| (Value of the capital stock on January 1, 1979) | (Amount of new investment undertaken during 1979) | (Depreciation for 1979) | (Value of the capital stock on January 1, 1980) |

These concepts may be more easily understood by comparing investment and depreciation to flows of water into and out of a tank, the contents of which represent the nation's stock of capital. In fact economists make a distinction between what they call flow variables and stock variables, the distinction depending upon the units of measurement. A flow variable is measured as a quantity per unit of time, a stock variable is simply a quantity. Thus wealth, measured in dollars, is a stock, while income, measured in dollars per year, is a flow. Capital is a stock; investment a flow. Other stock variables include the size of the labor force and the money supply. All of the variables depicted in Fig. 2-6 are flow variables. Figure 3-1 illustrates the relationship between investment, depreciation, and the capital stock in diagrammatic form.

The net addition to the capital stock, called net investment (I_n), is

---

3. This method of depreciating an asset is only one of many. It does have the merit of being the simplest, is perfectly adequate for explaining the concept of depreciation, and is therefore used here.

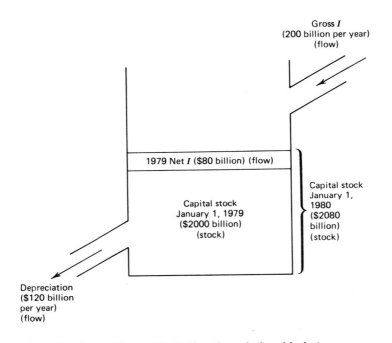

Gross *I*
(200 billion per year)
(flow)

1979 Net *I* ($80 billion) (flow)

Capital stock
January 1, 1979
($2000 billion)
(stock)

Capital stock
January 1,
1980
($2080
billion)
(stock)

Depreciation
($120 billion
per year)
(flow)

Figure 3-1. Stocks and flows illustrating the relationship between gross and net investment, depreciation, and the stock of capital.

the difference between the business sector's expenditure on new investment, gross investment (I_g), and depreciation.

$$I_n = I_g - \text{Depreciation}$$

In the simple economy we examined in Chapter 2, before the introduction of either a government or a foreign sector, all goods and services were either consumption or investment.

$$\text{GNP} = C + I$$

In the relationship above investment is defined in gross terms.

$$\text{GNP} = C + I_g$$

If we replace gross investment with net investment, we have another measure of the performance of the economy, net national product (NNP).

$$\text{NNP} = C + I_n$$

Suppose that in our previous example consumption were equal to $1500 billion. It follows that

$$\text{GNP} = \underset{\text{(Consumption)}}{\$1500 \text{ billion}} + \underset{\text{(Gross investment)}}{\$200 \text{ billion}} = \$1700 \text{ billion}$$

$$\text{NNP} = \underset{\text{(Consumption)}}{\$1500 \text{ billion}} + \underset{\text{(Net investment)}}{\$80 \text{ billion}} = \$1580 \text{ billion}$$

One other important relationship is easily derived

$$\text{GNP} - \text{NNP} = C + Ig - (C + I_n)$$

$$= I_g - I_n = \text{Depreciation}$$

Rearranging,

$$\text{NNP} = \text{GNP} - \text{Depreciation}$$

IV.   GNP AND NNP

Having two measures of the performance of our national economy, the question naturally arises as to which is the better. Clearly it is NNP. While both measures include consumption—there is no difference between them in that regard—NNP reflects the net addition to the stock of capital and thus gives a better picture of the economy's ability to produce goods and services in the following year.

Having said this, another question arises. Why is it that whenever economic matters are discussed in the news media, the commentators always focus on GNP and almost never mention NNP at all?

First, GNP is much easier to compute. Although monthly figures often have to be revised as more exact data come to light, quite good estimates for each month (multiplied by twelve to put the figure on an annual basis) and quarter (multiplied by four in a similar fashion) are available fairly soon after the end of each period. Good estimates of depreciation are harder to find.

Second, what we are really interested in most of the time is the rate of increase (or decrease) in the output of the economy. GNP and NNP tend to move together since depreciation changes relatively slowly. Should GNP increase by 8 percent, for example, NNP will increase by some amount fairly close to that. For this purpose, then, GNP is just as useful a measure as NNP and has become familiar to people who are not economists, while NNP is a term reserved almost exclusively for economists.

Although GNP appears center-stage when the economy is under discussion, it does suffer from some serious defects as a measure of the economy's performance. Consider a paper mill that produces $3 million worth of paper in a year. GNP will reflect the value of the paper, but not of the pollution of the stream on which the mill is located, nor of the air downwind from its chimney stack. GNP over-states the social value of the mill's activities. Alternatively, if the owners of the mill ensure that pollution is held to a minimum, their expenditures on pollution control are included in GNP. While the environment in their neighborhood is not much worse than it was before the mill was constructed, it is not much better either. Insofar as society is concerned, the environmental situation is unchanged, yet GNP is greater than it otherwise would be by the amount of the mill's expenditures on pollution control.

Or visualize a serious epidemic of some strange new disease sweeping the country. Expenditures on health care would skyrocket, and GNP would increase by a like amount. Yet it is impossible to argue that these expenditures represent a net social benefit. We would be much better off if the epidemic had never appeared in the first place.

Again, while real GNP per capita was over 6.7 times as great in 1970 as it was in 1870, the 1970 figure understates the increase in the quality of life that has occurred in the past 100 years. Output in 1876 was produced by a labor force that toiled for 10 hours per day, for 6 days a week—a work week of 60 hours, often of hard manual labor. In 1970 the 5-day 40-hour week was almost universal, and machines performed or assisted in performing the tasks that had previously fallen to the labor force. Yet the GNP figures give no hint of the social benefits of increased leisure that we have experienced over the last century.

GNP is an unsatisfactory measure of our economy's performance, yet so far all attempts to come up with a meaningful and acceptable alternative have failed. GNP is a poor measure, but it is the best we have.

Referring back to Fig. 2-3, that simplified figure did not take de-preciation into account at all. Now that we have introduced the concept, we must decide whether the I component of $C + I$ in the top flow should be I_g or I_n. It is I_n. To see why, recall that the bottom flow, or national income, is equal to the sum of wages, interest, rent, and profits. Depreciation represents a cost over and above the first three of these, which is subtracted from business receipts before arriving at the profit figure on the bottom line of the account. Since the bottom flow does not contain depreciation, it must not appear in the top flow either if we want the two flows to remain equal. We need net investment, and the top flow represents NNP. It follows therefore that:

$$NNP = NI$$

V. THE GOVERNMENT SECTOR

As we saw in the previous chapter, the inclusion in our analysis of a government sector gives us an additional injection (government spending), an additional leakage (taxes), and a third variable that simply represents the taking of money from one pocket of the household sector and placing it in another (transfer payments). Let us examine each in turn.

A. Government Spending

First thoughts might lead one to question the need for a separate component of GNP to be given the symbol G. After all, building a new post office, or a new superhighway, represents expenditures on construction, and thus by definition on investment. Similarly, it might be argued, mail delivery to a private household is consumption. In contrast, consider the operation of the National Park Service. It provides recreational opportunities for the millions of people who visit the parks each year; expenditures on the parks might be considered consumption. At the same time, the rangers who safeguard the trees within the park boundaries are conserving, indeed enhancing, a resource that may one day be an important input to the timber industry. Seen in this light, the expenditures represent investment. Because examples such as this one are the rule, rather than the exception, the national income accountants make an attempt to separate C from I. All expenditures by government are G.

B. Taxes

Economists classify taxes in a variety of ways. One of the simplest of divisions is into direct and indirect taxes. A direct tax is one that falls directly on income. The two major direct taxes are the personal income tax, which falls directly on personal income—on the income of the household sector—and the corporate profits tax, which bears directly on corporate profits—on the income of the business sector. An indirect tax, by contrast, is one that does not tax income directly. Two examples are the sales tax, a tax on consumption, and the property tax, a tax on wealth.

   Another useful method of classification is into taxes paid by users of a service provided by government and those based on ability to pay. An example of the former is the tax paid at airports by airline passengers. When a new airport is constructed by a city government, equity dictates that the cost be borne by the people who use the facility, and not by the nonflying residents of the city. Further, the amount of the cost that is borne should increase with the amount of use. A tax of, say $3 on each airline ticket purchased meets these requirements exactly.

In contrast to a new airport, which is used by only a limited number of people, the national defense protects us all. How should the cost of maintaining the armed serves be financed? A common method is to base each person's contribution on the ability to pay. The rich pay more than the poor. This concept leads us to yet a third means of subdividing taxes, by looking at how the ratio of tax (T) to income changes as income changes. If the amount of tax paid is always the same fraction of income, the tax is proportional. If the fraction increases as income increases, the tax is progressive; if it decreases, the tax is regressive.[4] These relationships are shown diagrammatically in Fig. 3-2.

This method of classification has important implications for government policymakers. If one of their goals is a more equal distribution of income, as we discussed in Chapter 1, then the tax structure should be progressive.

A fourth method of tax taxonomy is based on the level of government that levies the tax. This gives us a division into federal, state, and local taxes. The most important source of federal taxes, in quantitative terms, is the personal income tax. The state governments rely heavily on the sales tax, while at the local level the most important source of funds is the property tax.

C. Transfer Payments

Funds taken from the household sector in the form of payroll taxes and channeled to the unemployed, to recipients of welfare payments and Social Security retirement benefits, and to those eligible for Medicare and Medicaid are known as transfer payments. Unlike other forms of government expenditures, transfer payments are not counted as part of the GNP. Their major function is to provide a minimum level of support for the economically weaker members of society. Although not all retired people are disadvantaged, many subsist on what they receive from these sources, and unemployment benefits provide a floor under the incomes of workers suffering from a temporary bout of unemployment. For those who are unemployed

---

4. Students with a knowledge of calculus will recognize that taxes are proportional, progressive, or regressive, as $d(T/Y)/dy$ is $= 0$, >0, or <0.

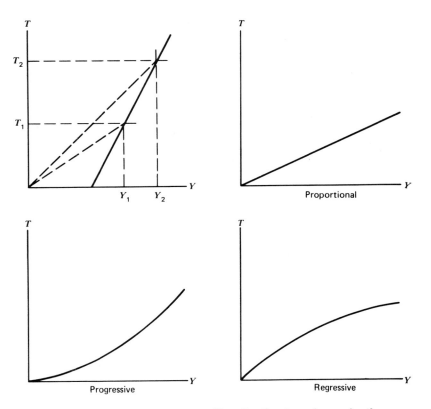

Figure 3.2.   Three kinds of taxes. Classify the tax shown in the upper left-hand diagram. Note that when Y increases from Y_1 to Y_2, T/Y, the slope of the line drawn from the origin, increases. The tax is therefore progressive.

for longer periods of time, and for those unable to work at all, welfare payments take up the slack.

Unlike interest on a business loan, which represents a payment for the use of capital, interest on the national debt is treated as a transfer payment, and is not included in GNP. The rationale for this is that, at least until recent times, most of our national debt was incurred to finance military expenditures during wars. (The national income accountants treat war as a nonproductive activity, a view with which most of the Vietnam War generation will heartily agree.)

This rationale is no longer valid. Since 1972, in an era of peace, the national debt has more than doubled, from $437 billion to $839 billion,[5] yet the national income accountants still treat the interest on the national debt as a transfer payment.

5. Estimated figure for 1979. Source: *Economic Report of the President*, 1979, pp. 264–265.

VI.   THE NATIONAL INCOME ACCOUNTS

Where does the production of an automobile in Detroit show up in the national income accounts? If it is sold to a private citizen for personal use, it represents consumption. If it is purchased by an insurance company to be driven by one of its salespeople, or if it becomes a net addition to inventory—on the floor of a dealer's showroom, for example—it represents investment. If it is part of a fleet purchase by a state government, it represents government spending, while if delivery is taken by a German citizen to speed along the Autobahn, it shows up in the account under the heading of exports. Since this exhausts all possibilities, it might appear that in general we can write:

$$Y = C + I + G + X$$

where the symbol Y stands for GNP if I is taken to mean gross investment, NNP if net, and X represents exports. But this is not so. Once we admit the existence of a foreign sector, and we do by the inclusion of exports, then we must also admit the possibility of imports.

Thus C may include the purchase of a Japanese camera, or of a flight on a Swissair jet; I may include the cost of a specialized machine manufactured in Sweden; G may be the purchase of supplies by an American embassy abroad. To the extent that C, I, and G include these imports, they overstate the production of goods by the American economy. To get the true figure for GNP (or NNP), therefore, imports (M) must be subtracted from the expression above.

$$Y = C + I + G + X - M$$

With the inclusion of a government sector, NNP is no longer equal to NI. A part of the circular flow is diverted from the business sector to the government sector in the form of sales or property taxes paid by business firms, more generally in the form of indirect business taxes (IBT). Thus,

$$NI = NNP - IBT$$

We now have two ways of calculating NNP. The method discussed earlier in the chapter

$$NNP = GNP - Depreciation$$

measures NNP *at market prices.* The second, just introduced,

$$NNP = NI + IBT$$

measures it *at factor cost.*

National income does not represent the amount that the household sector has available for spending. The business sector retains some of its profits to finance investment, a form of business saving, also known as retained earnings.

Retained earnings = Corporate profits after taxes − Dividends

Contributions to social insurance, both by the employer and the employee, must also be subtracted. Some other items not included in GNP, and hence not in NI, do represent income to the household sector and must be added. The most important ones are transfer payments and interest on the national debt. After these adjustments have been made to NI, we have another measure of the income of the household sector, personal income (PI).

$$PI = NI - \left[\begin{array}{c} \text{Corporate} \\ \text{Profits} \end{array} + \begin{array}{c} \text{Employer and Employee} \\ \text{contributions for} \\ \text{social insurance} \end{array} + \begin{array}{c} \text{Corporate} \\ \text{income} \\ \text{taxes} \end{array} \right]$$

$$+ \left[\begin{array}{c} \text{Transfer} \\ \text{Payments} \end{array} + \begin{array}{c} \text{Interest on the} \\ \text{national debt} \end{array} + \begin{array}{c} \text{Corporate} \\ \text{dividends} \end{array} \right]$$

Subtracting personal taxes from PI gives disposable personal income (DPI)—"takehome pay."

$$DPI = PI - \text{Personal taxes}$$

Finally, DPI may be either consumed or saved.

$$DPI = C + S$$

VII.   REAL VERSUS MONEY FLOWS: CURRENT OR CONSTANT DOLLARS

Another problem we must now face arises from the use of the dollar flow to measure the output of the economy. While this procedure has the tremendous advantage of enabling us to add up the many diverse goods and services that are produced, there is a corresponding disadvantage involving the unit of measurement we have chosen: the dollar. Unlike units of length, weight, or capacity, which do not vary, the value of the dollar does. If you measured the length of a room on January 1 and found it to be 16 feet 2 inches, you would be extremely surprised to discover that it was only 14 feet 10 inches on the first of June. On the other hand, the experience of recent years has probably caused you to become resigned to the fact that the dollar bill that purchased four hamburgers in 1970 will only exchange for two in 1980. The use of the dollar as the unit for economic measurement is certainly convenient, but it does cause problems because of the variability in its value. Again the solution is best introduced by means of a simplified example.

Imagine the tropical island of Paradisium, whose inhabitants' diet consists entirely of the fruit of the papaya tree. Suppose that their currency is called the dollar, and that one hundred cents equal one dollar, just as they do in the United States. The island's major economic statistics for 1978 and 1979 are shown in Table 3-1.

Table 3-1 Economic Statistics for Paradisium, 1978 and 1979

	OUTPUT OF PAPAYAS	GNP IN DOLLARS
1978	4000	800
1979	?	1000

It is readily seen that in 1978 the average price of papayas was $0.20, or, and it is equally valid to express the relationship between the dollar and the papaya in this fashion, one dollar was worth five papayas. How are we to interpret the 1979 GNP of $1000?

If the relationship between the dollar and the papaya does not change, it indicates that 5000 papayas were produced in that year, enabling the inhabitants of Paradisium to consume 25 percent more food than they did in 1978. Clearly their standard of living has risen. Their real GNP—that is, their GNP as measured in dollars of the same purchasing power as in the previous year—has also increased by 25 percent. Because the relationship between the dollar and the papaya is unchanged, it does not matter whether we base the calculation on the fact that the production of papayas has increased from 4000 to 5000, or that the dollar value of those papayas has increased from 800 to 1000; the result is the same increase of 25 percent.

But the figures in Table 2-3 are also consistent with the output of papayas remaining constant at 4000 per year. In that case the increased GNP must reflect a change in the price of papayas, from $0.20 to $0.25 each. While the standard of living of the Paradisians has not changed, they have experienced inflation at an annual rate of 25 percent.[6] Put in another way, the value of the Paradisian dollar has declined from five papayas to four.

We have now examined two extreme cases: one in which the increase in GNP is due entirely to a change in real output and one in which it is due entirely to a change in the price level. The in-between case is perhaps more usual. Just one possibility is illustrated in Table 3-2.

Table 3-2 Economic Statistics for Paradisium, 1970 and 1971

	OUTPUT OF PAPAYAS	GNP IN DOLLARS
1970	2000	200
1971	2100	252

While real output has increased in one year by 5 percent, GNP as measured in current dollars has risen by 26 percent. The difference is due to a change in the price level. In 1970 the average price of papayas was $0.10; in 1971 it was $0.12. Inflation occurred at an annual rate of 20 percent.

We need some means of measuring the increase in real GNP that will serve when we move to the economies of the real world, where many more goods than papayas are produced and consumed. The problem arises from the fact that the dollar in which 1970's GNP was measured was worth more than its 1971 counterpart.

The solution is to measure GNP for both years in dollars of the same value, either 1970 dollars or 1971 dollars. If we choose 1970 as the base year, the price index for that year will be 100, representing 100 percent of 1970's price level. The price index for 1971 will be

$$100 \times \frac{\$0.12}{\$0.10} = 120$$

Therefore the 1971 dollar value of GNP must be deflated (because 1971 dollars are worth less than 1970 dollars) in the ratio 100/120 making the 1971 GNP, as measured in 1970 dollars,

$$\$252 \times \frac{100}{120} = \$210$$

It is equally permissible to measure both years' GNPs in terms of 1971 dollars. This time 1971's price index is 100, and 1970's will be

$$100 \times \frac{\$0.10}{\$0.12} = 83.3$$

6. An obvious implicit assumption here is that the population of Paradisium has remained constant. Strictly speaking, an increase in the price of only one product does not constitute inflation. In this very special case in which only one good is produced, an increase in the price of one good means an increase in the price of all goods. That is inflation.

Hence the 1970 figure must be inflated (because 1970 dollars are worth more than 1971 dollars) in the ratio 100/83.3, making the 1970 GNP, as measured in 1971 dollars,

$$\$200 \times \frac{100}{83.3} = \$240$$

These results are summarized in Table 3-3.

Table 3-3 Economic Statistics for Paradisium, 1970 and 1971

GNP MEASURED IN CURRENT DOLLARS		REAL GNP	
		1970 DOLLARS	1971 DOLLARS
1970	200	200	240
1971	252	210	252

It will be observed that it does not matter which year is chosen as the base year; the increase in real GNP is 5 percent, confirming the earlier calculation. The figures in the second column may be expressed in either of two ways: (1) money GNP rose from $200 to $252; or (2) GNP in current dollars rose from 200 to 252. The results in the third column may also be given in two ways: (1) real GNP increased from $200 to $210; or (2) GNP in constant dollars increased from 200 to 210. For completeness one should add that the dollars in question are 1970 dollars; 1970 is the base year and the price index for that year is 100.

When the year-to-year changes are small, and an approximate answer will serve, the calculation becomes much simpler. Suppose that real GNP and the price index are both 100. Suppose further that in the following year real GNP has increased by X percent and that the inflation rate is Y percent. Money GNP will have increased to

$$100 \left(1 + \frac{X}{100} \right) \left(1 + \frac{Y}{100} \right) =$$

$$100 \left(1 + \frac{X}{100} + \frac{Y}{100} + \frac{XY}{100^2} \right)$$

Since X and Y are both small, $XY/10,000$ is extremely small when compared to 1, $X/100$, and $Y/100$, and may be dropped out without causing any significant error. Hence in the second year

$$\text{Money GNP} = 100 + X + Y$$

The percentage increase in money GNP, $X + Y$, is the sum of the percentage increase in real GNP and the percentage rate of inflation. By way of example, suppose that real GNP increases by 5 percent and the rate of inflation is 3 percent; money GNP will increase by

$$5 + 3 = 8 \text{ percent}$$

In our earlier example (Table 2-5), real GNP increased by 5 percent, the rate of inflation was 20 percent, and the increase in money GNP was 26 percent. In this case,

$$5 + 20 = 25 \neq 26$$

The numbers do not add up exactly because the rate of inflation, 20 percent, is not a small number.

A. Extension of the Analysis to the Production of Two Goods

Now we may introduce one more level of complexity. The neighboring island of Pacificum has a less equitable climate. Its inhabitants not only produce papayas for food, but also silk for clothing. Pacificum's statistics are shown in Table 3-4.

Table 3-4 Economic Statistics for Pacificum, 1978 and 1979

| | OUTPUT OF: | | DOLLAR VALUE OF: | | |
	PAPAYAS	SILK (YARDS)	PAPAYAS	SILK	GNP
1978	700	3500	70	700	770
1979	900	6000	126	1260	1386

It is readily calculated that the price of papayas in 1978 was $0.10; silk was $0.20 per yard. In 1979 the corresponding figures were $0.14 and $.21. The price of papayas has thus risen by 40 percent in one year, while that of silk has increased by 5 percent. How do these changes affect the overall price level?

It is apparent at once that a simple average, 22.5 percent, will not do. That gives equal weight to changes in the prices of both papayas and silk, whereas it is clear that silk is much the more important of the two commodities to the Pacificans. We need to calculate the average of the two price increases, but it must be a weighted average, with the weights depending on the fraction of the GNP that the output of each commodity represents. Fortunately, in each of the two years the Pacificans spent one-eleventh of their incomes on papayas and ten-elevenths on silk. These, then, are the appropriate weights to use, and the price index for 1979 (1978 = 100) is thus

$$140 \times \frac{1}{11} + 105 \times \frac{10}{11} = \frac{140 + 1050}{11} = \frac{1190}{11} = 108.2$$

and the inflation rate is 8.2 percent.

B. Extension of the Analysis to the Real World

The calculation of a price index in the more complex real world, where many different goods and services are produced, is much more difficult. A price index is a weighted average of the prices of all the commodities on which it is based, with the weights being determined by the relative importance of the commodities in question. In constructing the consumer price index, for example, which reflects the items the average householder purchases during the course of a year, a much larger weight is given to the price of automobiles, on which a fairly large proportion of household income is spent, than to the price of salt, which makes an insignificant dent in the household budget.

As may be imagined, the problem is actually even more complex than we have so far indicated, even in the very simple economy of Pacificum. It is most unlikely that every year the islanders spend exactly one-eleventh of their income on papayas and ten-elevenths on silk. Suppose that in 1979 they actually spent one-tenth on papayas and nine-tenths on silk. Which would be the appropriate weights to use, the 1978 or the 1979 ratios?

Or suppose that in 1979 the higher price for silk reflected, in part, an increase in quality, so that the silk produced in that year was actually a better product that that of 1978. Living standards would rise, even if the number of yards of silk produced remained unchanged. But by how much? Judgments have to be made on these and other matters, judgments that would take us beyond the scope of an elementary text.

One thing can be said, however. The types of change we have just discussed take time. Spending habits do not change much in one year, but may differ significantly between the beginning and the end of a decade, or of a half-century. A 1979 model car may not be significantly better (or worse) than a 1978 model, but it is clearly a different mechanism than a model of the 1920s. Thus we are on fairly safe ground in comparing 1979's price index to 1978's; the comparison is much less meaningful if made with the index for 1929.

VIII.   THE NATIONAL INCOME ACCOUNTS FOR THE UNITED STATES: THE MAGNITUDE OF THE VARIABLES

The analysis in this, and the previous chapter, was carried out at a theoretical level, supplemented with some statistics for the hypothetical economies of Paradisium and Pacificum. It is also important to get some sort of feel for the magnitude of the variables in recent times in the United States. The latest available figures when this was written were for the year 1978.[7] In billions of dollars,

$$\text{GNP} = C + I_g + G + X - M$$

$$2106.6 \quad 1339.7 \quad 344.5 \quad 434.2 \quad 205.2 \quad 217.0$$

$$\text{GNP} = \text{NNP} + \text{Depreciation}$$

$$2106.6 \quad 1889.7 \quad 216.9$$

$$\text{NI} = 1703.6 \qquad \text{PI} = 1707.3$$

$$\text{DPI} = 1451.2$$

The record of growth rates and inflation for the past nine years is contained in Table 3-5.

Table 3-5 United States Statistics, 1970–1978

| | CHANGE IN GNP FROM PRECEEDING PERIOD% | | |
	MEASURED IN CURRENT DOLLARS	MEASURED IN 1972 DOLLARS	RATE OF INFLATION, %
1970	5.0	−0.3	5.4
1971	8.2	3.0	5.1
1972	10.1	5.7	4.1
1973	11.6	5.5	5.8
1974	8.1	−1.4	9.7
1975	8.2	−1.3	9.6
1976	11.2	5.7	5.2
1977	11.0	4.9	5.9
1978	11.6	3.9	7.4

7. Source: *Economic Report of the President, 1979.* Figures may not add up exactly because of rounding.

It is apparent that the major component of GNP is consumption. In 1978 over 63 percent of GNP was consumption (*C*). If we wish to know what determines the level of GNP in a particular time period, we are over halfway there if we know what determines *C*. That will be the focus of the next chapter.

IX.   SUMMARY AND CONCLUSION

In order to make the concept more meaningful, consumption is defined to include some nonmonetary transactions that are considered important: the value of goods produced and consumed on the farm, the value of a free checking account, and the rental value of an owner-occupied home. Items that are excluded include the services of a homemaker and the fruits of illegal activities.

Investment represents additions to the nation's stock of capital. Gross investment is the dollar value of the output of capital goods in a given year. Net investment is equal to gross investment less depreciation. In GNP the investment component is defined in gross terms; in NNP it is net.

Government spending is defined as the sum of all expenditures by government, except transfer payments. Taxes generate government receipts, while transfer payments, which are not counted as a component of GNP, are designed to give some minimum level of income to the disadvantaged.

While the use of the dollar as a unit of measurement leads to a valuable simplificiation of the model that makes it easier to understand, a problem arises from the fact that the dollar does not have a constant value. The use of "constant" dollars, or real measures of economic variables, is one way to overcome this problem.

QUESTIONS

1. The capital stock of Ruritania on January 1, 1970, was $300,000. During the year gross investment was $60,000, depreciation $20,000 and consumption $800,000.
   (a)   What was the value of the capital stock on January 1, 1971?
   (b)   What was net investment for 1970?
   (c)   Calculate GNP in 1970.
   (d)   Calculate NNP in 1970.
2. Which of the following taxes are direct? Indirect? Which represent a tax on users of a government service?
   (a)   Personal income tax.
   (b)   Sales tax.
   (c)   Business property taxes.
   (d)   Corporate profits tax.
   (e)   Tax proportional to the quantity of water used each month.
   (f)   Excise tax on cigarettes.

3.

Table 3-6 Economic Statistics for Paradisium, 1940 and 1941

YEAR	GNP IN CURRENT DOLLARS	PRICE INDEX (1940 * 100)	INDEX (1941 * 100)	REAL GNP 1940 DOLLARS	GNP 1941 DOLLARS
1940	120	100	_80_	120	——— _156_
1941	200	125	100	_130_	200

(a) Copy Table 3-6 and fill in the blank spaces.
(b) What was the percentage rate of growth in money GNP (1940–1941)?
(c) What was the rate of inflation (1940–1941)?
(d) What was the rate of growth in real GNP (1940–1941)?
(e) Calculate the sum of (c) and (d).
(f) Why do the answers to (b) and (e) differ?

Prices Rose 25%

GNP Current Rose 2/3

$\frac{125}{100} = 1,25$

$\frac{100}{x} = 1,25$

$x = 1,25 \overline{)1,00\,00}$

4 | The Keynesian Consumption Function

Prior to the widespread acceptance of Keynesian macroeconomics, economists were not terribly interested in consumption. If pressed, they would probably say that it was determined somewhat as follows. With the economy operating at the full employment level, real income is fixed in the short run. In a simple model without a government sector:

$$Y = C + S$$

where Y = NNP = NI = DPI and all variables are measured in real terms.

The level of saving depends on the rate of interest—a higher rate of interest encouraging more saving and a lower rate inducing less. Since consumption is the part of income that is not saved, consumption declines with rising interest rates and increases as they fall. In a world where income stays relatively constant, we must look to the rate of interest to determine the level of consumption.

I. THE KEYNESIAN APPROACH

Keynes took the approach outlined above and stood it on its head. Income is not fixed at the full-employment level, he argued, and saving is influenced very little, if at all, by the level of interest rates.[1]

---

1. Before reading further, you might get some perspective on these opposing views by imagining that you are employed at a salary of $800 per month. Try to estimate how much of that income you would save if the interest rate paid on your savings were 4 percent. Now attempt to answer two questions: (1) How much more would you save if the interest paid were increased to 6 percent, your income remaining constant? (2) How much more would you save if your income were increased to $1200 per month, the interest rate remaining constant?

Income determines saving and consumption, which both increase when income does.[2] Let us examine each of these propositions in turn.

II.   THE RELATIONSHIP BETWEEN SAVING AND INTEREST RATES

Some individuals, it is true, save more as the interest rate rises. This statement is particularly true of negative savers. Borrowing may be regarded as negative saving, since borrowing pushes one deeper into debt, while (positive) saving reduces one's debts. Almost everyone thinks twice about incurring more debt when the interest rate—the cost of borrowing—is high, but they lightheartedly buy on credit when it is low.

But consider the woman who wants to save $10,000 to make a down payment on a beauty shop in eight years. That $10,000 will be made up of two components; the amount she saves and the interest she receives. If interest rates rise, the interest component increases. She need not save as much as when interest rates were lower. In other words, a rise in the interest rate causes her to save less.

Do many people behave in this fashion? First thoughts are that the individual pattern of behavior cited above is rather rare. In actuality it is widespread. Life insurance represents saving, since money is put away today, in the form of premiums, to be paid back in the future, at the death of the insured person, at the age of sixty-five, or after some agreed time span. The insurance companies invest these premiums at interest and pay a portion of the proceeds to their clients in the form of "dividends." Dividends increase when interest rates rise and decline when they fall. Since dividends are in effect equivalent to a reduction in the premium, and since the premium represents saving, it is apparent that an increase in interest rates leads to a decrease in this particular type of saving.

With some groups saving more as the interest rate rises and others saving less, the net effect is that aggregate saving is influenced little, if at all, by changes in the interest rate. Neither, therefore, is consumption.

III.   THE FAMILY CONSUMPTION FUNCTION: THE GEOMETRY

Think first of a single family unit, and try to decide how much it would spend on consumption at varying levels of income. This

---

2. Opponents of the Keynesian view would not have disagreed with this statement, but would have regarded it as uninteresting because they did not believe that income changed very much in the short run.

relationship between consumption and income is called—the name is from Keynes—the consumption function. Even with an income of zero, the family needs some minimal level of consumption to stay alive. If we rule out recourse to illegal activities, such consumption can only be financed by borrowing. Figure 4-1 depicts this level at $2000 per year. When the family receives some small amount of income we may visualize it as doing two things: (1) increasing its consumption expenditures, and (2) reducing the amount it borrows. The diagram shows that with an income of $4000 the family purchases goods and services worth $5000. Its consumption has increased from $2000 to $5000, and the amount of borrowing needed to finance its expenditures has declined from $2000 to $1000. As its income increases further, so too does consumption, while the need to borrow becomes less and less urgent. Indeed, at an income of $8000, the diagram shows consumption of exactly the same amount. Above that level, consumption is financed entirely out of income; $8000 is the family's break-even point. At higher incomes the family no longer needs to spend all of its income. At $12,000 per year, for example, consumption expenditures are only $11,000. The family is saving $1000 per year.

The consumption function of Fig. 4-1 was put together intuitively, but it does not differ too much from one derived from a study of real-life families. A minor difference: our function is linear; in real life it has some degree of curvature (Fig. 4-2). Following Keynes, we will stay with the linear function, because of both the advantage of simplicity and the fact that we are almost invariably interested in what happens to consumption as a result of a small change in income. Although the function in Fig. 4-2 is curved, the short portion lying between incomes of, say, $10,000 and $12,000 per year may be treated in our analysis as being approximately a straight line.

The Keynesian view of the consumption function, while the first in point of time, is today only one among several competing hypotheses. To distinguish it from these other hypotheses, it is sometimes called the *absolute-income hypothesis,* since consumption depends on the absolute level of income, as distinguished from, for example, the level of one family's income in relation to another's (see Chapter 12).

IV. THE MARGINAL AND AVERAGE PROPENSITIES TO CONSUME

In Fig. 4-1, when income increases from $8000 to $9000 per year, consumption in the same time period increases from $8000 to $8750. The ratio

$$\frac{\Delta C}{\Delta Y} = \frac{\$(8750 - 8000)}{\$(9000 - 8000)} = 0.75$$

is called the marginal propensity to consume (MPC). The symbol Δ means "a small change in. . . ." Thus ΔC represents a small change in C. The ratio $\Delta C/\Delta Y$ is, in terms of geometry, the slope of the consumption function. Because our consumption function is a straight line, it has a constant slope; the MPC is the same at all levels of income. In Fig. 4-2, on the other hand, the MPC declines as income increases.

When income is $12,000 per year, consumption is $11,000. The ratio of these two numbers

$$\frac{C}{Y} = \frac{\$11,000}{\$12,000} = 0.92$$

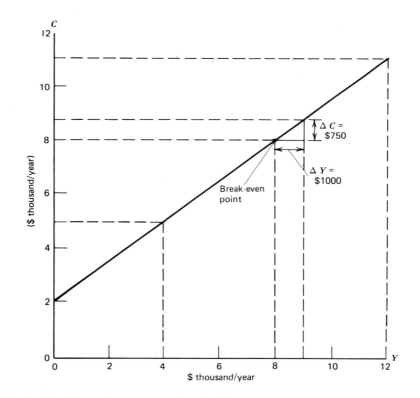

Figure 4-1. Keynesian consumption function.

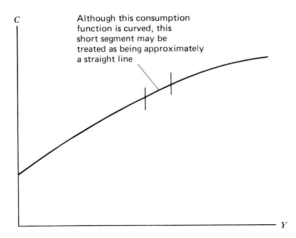

Figure 4-2. Shape of the consumption function derived from a study of real-life families.

is known as the average propensity to consume (APC). Unlike the corresponding marginal propensity, the APC is not constant, but declines continuously as income increases. C/Y at any point on the consumption function is the slope of a line drawn from the origin to that point and, as Fig. 4-3 shows, that line gets less and less steep as we move farther and farther along the income axis.

One other relationship is of some importance. The slope of a line from the origin to any point on the function meets the function from below (Fig. 4-3 again). Its slope is always greater than the slope of the consumption function itself, which in turn means that

$$APC > MPC$$

In economic terms, these results mean that while the rich consume a smaller fraction of their income than do the poor, both groups consume the same (lesser) fraction of an increment in income.

V. THE FAMILY CONSUMPTION FUNCTION: THE ALGEBRA

The consumption function illustrated in Fig. 4-1 has the following algebraic form:

$$C = 2000 + 0.75Y$$

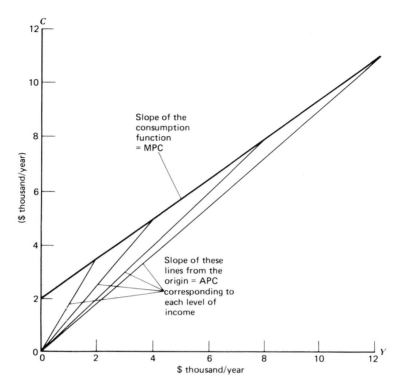

Figure 4-3. Illustrating MPC and APC and the relationship between them geometrically.

both variables being measured in dollars. The intercept term is $2000, the level of consumption when income is zero, and the slope of the consumption function, the coefficient of Y, is 0.75.

To derive the break-even point, put $Y = C$—that is,

$$Y = 2000 + 0.75Y$$

whence

$$0.25Y = 2000 \quad \text{or} \quad Y = 8000$$

$$APC = \frac{C}{Y} = \frac{2000 + 0.75Y}{Y}$$

$$= 0.75 + \frac{2000}{Y}$$

Since Y is nonnegative, APC declines as Y increases. Since MPC = 0.75,

$$\text{APC} = \text{MPC} + \frac{2000}{Y}$$

APC is always greater than MPC by some positive number; hence,

$$\text{APC} > \text{MPC}$$

as before.

VI. THE SAVING FUNCTION: THE GEOMETRY

Once we know what the consumption function looks like, the corresponding saving function is readily derived. Figure 4-4 is simply a replica of Fig. 4-1 with the addition of a 45-degree line starting at the origin. This line has the property that the perpendicular distance from any point on it to the Y-axis is exactly the same as the corresponding distance to the C-axis (the construct is important, we will use it again later). Figure 4-4 shows that a vertical line drawn from the 45-degree line to intersect the horizontal axis at the point Y = 4000 also has a length, as measured on the vertical C-axis, of 4000. Since

$$Y = C + S$$

or

$$S = Y - C$$

it follows that the vertical distance between the 45-degree line and the consumption function represents saving. For example, when Y = \$10,000, C = \$9500, the vertical distance from the Y-axis to the consumption function, and S = \$500, the vertical distance between the consumption function and the 45-degree line.

When Y = \$0, C of \$2000 is financed entirely by borrowing. Since, as we saw, borrowing is equivalent to negative saving, S = −\$2000. At the break-even point of Y = \$8000, S = \$0 since the saving function crosses the Y-axis at this point. These points have been plotted on the lower part of Fig. 4-4. It only takes two points to determine a straight line; the saving function is drawn through those two points.

VII. THE MARGINAL AND AVERAGE PROPENSITIES TO SAVE

When Y increases from \$8000 to \$10,000, S increases from \$0 to \$500. The slope of the saving function

$$\frac{\Delta S}{\Delta Y} \;=\; \frac{\$500}{\$2000} \;=\; 0.25$$

is known as the marginal propensity to save (MPS). The average propensity to save (APS = S/Y) is negative for all Y less than \$8000, is

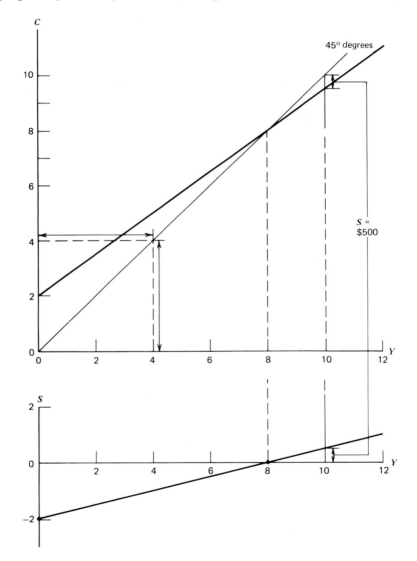

Figure 4-4. Derivation of the saving function.
(All variables are measured in thousands of dollars per year.)

zero for $Y = \$8000$, and is positive for all Y greater than $\$8000$. Like the corresponding propensity to consume, it may be represented geometrically by the slope of a line drawn from the origin to the appropriate point on the saving function. Since the slope of this line is always less than the slope of the saving function itself, it follows that

$$\text{APS} < \text{MPS}$$

VIII.   THE SAVING FUNCTION: THE ALGEBRA

Substituting $C = 2000 + 0.75Y$ in $Y = C + S$ leads to

$$Y = 2000 + 0.75Y + S$$

whence

$$S = -2000 + 0.25Y$$

the equation of the saving function.

The intercept on the S-axis is -2000, and the slope of the function, the coefficient of Y $(= 0.25)$ is the MPS.

$$\text{APS} = \frac{S}{Y} = \frac{-2000 + 0.25Y}{Y} = 0.25 - \frac{2000}{Y}$$

Since Y is nonnegative, the APS increases as Y increases. Further, since $\text{MPS} = 0.25$,

$$\text{APS} = \text{MPS} - \frac{2000}{Y}$$

APS is always less than MPS by some positive number; hence,

$$\text{APS} < \text{MPS}$$

IX.   THE RELATIONSHIPS BETWEEN THE SAVING AND CONSUMPTION FUNCTIONS: THE GENERAL CASE

The consumption and saving functions we have just discussed may be generalized to

$$C = C_0 + cY \qquad\qquad S = S_0 + sY$$

where C_0 is the intercept on the C-axis of the consumption function, and S_0 is the intercept on the S-axis of the saving function. It follows that $S_0 = {}^- C_0$. The coefficient c and s, the slopes of the consumption and saving functions, are the MPC and the MPS, respectively.

Since an increase in income is either consumed or saved,

$$\Delta Y = \Delta C + \Delta S$$

Dividing through by ΔY and rearranging,

$$\frac{\Delta C}{\Delta Y} + \frac{\Delta S}{\Delta Y} = \frac{\Delta Y}{\Delta Y}$$

Or

$$c + s = 1$$

The sum of the marginal propensities is equal to unity.

A similar result holds for the average propensities

$$Y = C + S$$

Dividing through by Y and rearranging,

$$\frac{C}{Y} + \frac{S}{Y} = 1$$

that is,

$$APC + APS = 1$$

Since the recipient of an increase in income might be expected to spend some of that increase, but not all of it,

$$0 < c < 1$$

It follows therefore that

$$0 < s < 1$$

X. THE AGGREGATE CONSUMPTION AND SAVING FUNCTIONS

The discussion of Sections III through IX has been couched in terms of the behavior of a single individual or of a family. We have examined the family functions.

In the next chapter we will deal with the relationship between aggregate consumption and aggregate income, and with the relationship between aggregate saving and aggregate income—with the aggregate functions.

The aggregate consumption function follows the same pattern as the family function. If one person has some positive level of consumption when income is zero, then so will all people. As income rises, so does consumption. The major difference is in the scale of the axes. Most individuals and families measure both consumption and income in thousands of dollars. In the aggregate, these variables are measured in billions, even hundreds of billions, of dollars.

Unlike the family consumption function, empirical studies have shown the aggregate function to be linear. There is some controversy over whether it does, or does not, start at the origin. For the moment we will retain the assumption of a positive intercept, postponing discussion of this particular controversy until Chapter 12.

These remarks about the aggregate consumption function also apply to the aggregate saving function. The latter may be derived from the former in much the same way that the family saving function was derived from the family consumption function.

The relationships that were derived between the average and marginal propensities are still valid for the aggregate functions. The results of the next chapter may be reached either by way of the aggregate consumption function or through the aggregate saving function. We will use both approaches.

XI. SUMMARY AND CONCLUSION

Unlike his predecessors, Keynes believed that saving depends on the level of income, not on the level of interest rates.

The consumption function depicts a relationship between consumption and income that is approximately linear with a positive intercept on the consumption axis and a constant slope equal to the marginal propensity to consume.

The saving function may be derived from the consumption function. It is also approximately linear with a positive slope equal to the marginal propensity to save, but has a negative intercept on the saving axis.

In macroeconomics we are usually more interested in the aggregate consumption and saving functions that follow a similar pattern to the family functions but have a much smaller scale on both axes.

QUESTIONS

1. With both variables measured in billions of dollars, the aggregate consumption function is

$$C = 2400 + 0.85Y$$

(a) Write the corresponding saving function.
(b) What is the MPC?
(c) What is the MPS?
(d) How can you check your answers to (b) and (c)?
     When $Y = 20,000$:
(e) What is the APC?
(f) What is the APS?
(g) How can you check your answers to (e) and (f)?
(h) Compare your answers to (b) and (e). Are they of the right order
     of magnitude? Why or why not? Now compare your answers to (c)
     and (f).
(i) What is the break-even point?

5 | What Determines GNP? The Keynesian Version

Figure 5-1 illustrates how the real gross national product has changed in the United States over a seventeen-year period. Several facets of the diagram strike the eye immediately.

First, GNP is growing. From a level of $799 billion in 1962, it increased to $1385 billion in 1978, both figures being expressed in constant 1972 dollars, an increase of 73 percent, and an average compounded rate of growth of 3.5 percent per annum.

Second, it does not grow at a uniform rate, but periods of rapid growth alternate with periods when growth is slower. Sometimes, although rarely, real GNP even declines. Real GNP in 1975, for example, was $33 billion less than it was in 1973.

The macroeconomist has three major questions to answer. (1) Why does GNP grow over time? This question takes us into the realms of growth theory, an extremely sophisticated and mathematical branch of economics. (2) Why does it fluctuate about the trend line? To answer that question requires a knowledge of business cycle theory. (3) Why was GNP in the year 1978 equal to $1385 billions of constant 1972 dollars? Keynes's answer to the third question is our next order of business.

I. SAVINGS AND INVESTMENT AGAIN

Keynes rejected the classic notion that the equality of saving and investment would always be brought about by the interest rate. First, as we saw in Chapter 4, there is some reason to believe that saving is unaffected by the rate of interest. Second, saving and investment are undertaken by different groups of people for different

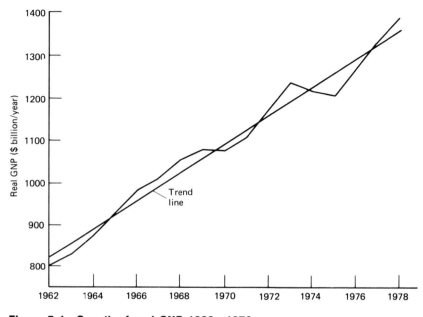

Figure 5-1. Growth of real GNP 1962–1978.
Source: *Economic Report of the President*, 1979, p. 184.

reasons: saving by the household sector and investment by the business sector. There is no reason why the plans of these two separate sectors should result in the equality of S and I.

In a deep depression businesspeople may not want to contemplate new investment at any rate of interest. Why should they when part of their existing stock of capital is idle? The relationship between saving, investment, and the rate of interest might therefore look something like that shown in Fig. 5-2.

To be sure, one might argue that the saving and investment functions do intersect at a negative rate of interest—minus 3 percent in the diagram.

But the rate of interest can never be negative. What does an interest rate of minus 3 percent mean? It means that the lender of $100 for one year is repaid $97 when the loan becomes due. Under such circumstances no one would be willing to lend money since a potential lender could always do better by putting a $100 bill in a safe-deposit box. At all positive rates of interest saving exceeds investment. Now let us tackle the question from a somewhat different viewpoint.

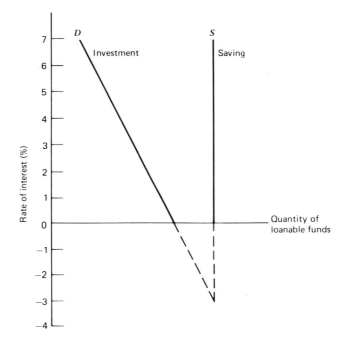

Figure 5-2. Failure of the rate of interest to equate saving and investment.

II.   INCOME DETERMINATION BY MEANS OF THE CONSUMPTION FUNCTION: THE GEOMETRY

Starting with the simple two-sector economy of Fig. 2-2, in which the top money flow (NNP) is equal to the bottom flow (NI), assume initially that the price level remains constant. Using the symbol Y to refer to both NNP and NI,

$$Y = C + I \qquad\qquad Y = C + S$$

$$\text{(NNP)} \qquad\qquad\quad \text{(NI)}$$

It follows that

$$C + I = C + S$$

and therefore that

$$S = I$$

This extremely important result presents us with a paradox. The heart of Keynesian theory, as we have just seen, is that saving and investment are not necessarily equal. Yet we have just shown that $S = I$ is a mathematical identity. The resolution of this paradox will, it turns out, provide us with the answer to the question of what determines the level of NNP and NI and hence, given some figure for depreciation, of GNP.

We now make a further simplifying assumption: that the level of investment in a given year is whatever businesspeople in the aggregate decide it should be. Each individual entrepreneur decides on the amount of investment that would be appropriate for the firm, and the sum of all these figures gives a total equal to I. It must be emphasized that these decisions are made separately; there is no discussion as to what the overall level of investment should be. At the same time, when economic conditions are favorable and optimism is widespread, most will be eager to expand; most firms' investment will be higher than usual, and so will the aggregate figure. When the economic skies turn gloomy, by contrast, retrenchment will be the order of the day, and investment will tend to be lower than normal.

Consumption follows the pattern of the Keynesian consumption function discussed in the previous chapter: C is a linear function of Y. That function is depicted in Fig. 5-3 and is labeled C.

Just as in microeconomics, we can construct a demand curve showing a relationship between the price of a commodity and the quantity purchased, holding income and the prices of other goods constant, so in macroeconomics we may think of an aggregate demand function. The Keynesian aggregate demand function, however, is a relationship between the value of the total quantity of goods and services that are purchased and national income, the price level being held constant.

Aggregate demand is equal to C (purchases by the household sector) + I (purchases by the business sector). It is a function of income since C is a function of income. Depicted in Fig. 5-3 by the line parallel to the consumption function at a vertical distance above it equal to I, it is labeled $C + I$.

Aggregate supply is the total quantity of goods and services produced by the business sector each year. Like investment, it is the sum of the thousands of output decisions made by individual firms. It is shown as a line from the origin at an angle of 45 degrees to the horizontal axis. Suppose, for example, that the business sector produces goods and services with a value of $800 billion, shown on the horizontal axis at point A. All the 45-degree line does is turn this horizontal measurement OA into an equal vertical distance AB (see Fig. 4-4 in Chapter 4).

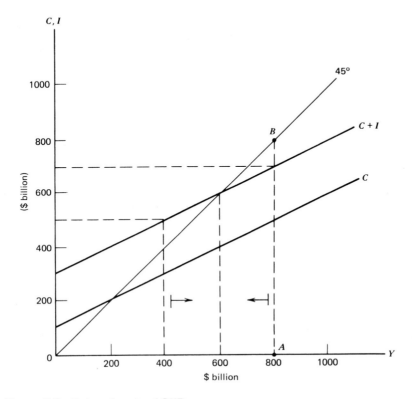

Figure 5-3. Determinants of GNP.

The production of $800 billion worth of goods and services generates an equivalent amount of income. With national income equal to $800 billion, aggregate demand may be read off from the $C + I$ line and is seen to be equal to $700 billion. Consumption alone is equal to $500 billion, meaning that saving is equal to $(800 -500 = 300)$ billion. Investment is equal to $200 billion. Saving and investment are clearly not equal. How can we reconcile this fact with our earlier demonstration of their equality?

The business sector produces $800 billion worth of goods and services, but sales amount to only $700 billion. Goods with a value of $100 billion remain unsold, on supermarket shelves, on the floors of automobile showrooms, in warehouses, and on farms. More generally, they represent a net addition to inventories, one of the components of investment.

Presumably the figure of $200 billion for investment includes some planned net addition to inventories,[1] but the $100 billion worth of unsold goods represents an addition over and above that, an unplanned addition. Actual—or realized—investment is $300 billion, consisting of $200 billion of planned investment plus a $100 billion unplanned increase in inventories. The paradox is resolved. Saving is equal to realized investment; both are $300 billion.

It is apparent that the business sector has made a misjudgment as to the quantity of goods it can sell. The way it moves to correct its error is an important link in the Keynesian chain.

Visualize an automobile dealer who likes to have thirty cars on the showroom floor to have sufficient variety to show to customers. The dealer finishes the year—or quarter, or month, or whatever the period of time between orders may be—with forty cars, because business has not been as good as expected. The dealer's reaction is to telephone the supplier in Detroit, asking that the number of cars shipped in the next time period be reduced. Receiving thousands of such calls from dealers around the country, automobile manufacturers cut back production and lay off workers. With similar cutbacks occurring in other industries, total output and employment decline. In terms of Fig. 5-3, Y declines to below $800 billion.

Now let us retrace our steps and consider what might happen if the business sector decided to produce goods and services with a total value of $400 billion. Aggregate demand will be $500 billion—more goods are purchased than are produced. At the end of the year our automobile dealer has only twenty cars on the showroom floor, and gets on the phone to ask Detroit to send a larger shipment of cars than usual. In response to this, and many other calls of a similar nature, the automakers step up production and hire more workers. Overall output and employment rise. Y increases to above $400 billion in the next time period.

To summarize, when $Y = $800 billion, forces are set into motion which tend to reduce it. When $Y = $400 billion, similar forces cause it to increase. Between those two figures one suspects that the forces no longer operate, just as a particle of iron remains stationary somewhere between the poles of a magnet.

Our suspicions are correct. When aggregate supply amounts to $600 billion, aggregate demand is equal to the same figure. There is no unintended inventory buildup or cutback. Businesspeople find their inventories at a comfortable level and continue to order new merchandise at the same rate as before. Clearly $600 billion is an

---

1. A planned net reduction is also possible. It would, of course, have a negative sign.

equilibrium level of Y; when it is there, no forces cause it to change. Furthermore, the equilibrium is stable; when Y is not equal to $600 billion, forces are set into motion that tend to move it toward that level.

As we saw earlier, saving is always equal to investment if investment is defined as realized investment. The equality of saving with planned investment only occurs at one level of Y: the equilibrium level.

The next step in the Keynesian argument is that there is no reason whatever, except pure coincidence, why that equilibrium should be one at which all resources are fully employed. With full employment of resources, let us assume that the economy is capable of producing goods and services with a total value of $800 billion per year. As we have just seen, once the economy reaches its equilibrium level of $600 billion it tends to stay there, producing at a level of $200 billion below its capacity. The people and machines that might have produced those goods and services are idle. The economy is in a deep depression and unemployment is rife.

Furthermore, since the equilibrium is stable, it does no good to sit back and wait for automatic forces to restore full employment. The automatic forces are at work, but they are working to keep Y at the $600 billion equilibrium level; they are working not to eliminate the unemployment situation, but to perpetuate it. No wonder that economists were excited by *The General Theory*. It seemed to account perfectly for the Great Depression of the 1930s and to explain precisely why it was so prolonged.

Now let us take a slightly different viewpoint. If the economy were in fact at the full-employment level of $800 billion, aggregate demand, as read from the $C + I$ line in Fig. 5-3, would be $700 billion. There is an insufficiency in aggregate demand equal to $100 billion, which results in a decline in Y to the equilibrium level of $600 billion. Insufficient demand leads to a deflationary situation,[2] hence the gap between the $C + I$ line and the 45-degree line, between aggregate demand and aggregate supply, is known as a deflationary gap.

Keynes was very much a man of his time, interested in finding an explanation for persistent unemployment, but the model he developed may also be used to account for inflation. If, with all re-

---

2. Deflation actually means a decline in the average price level, which is inconsistent with our initial assumption of a constant price level. Forces that would cause prices to fall if they were free to do so result in unemployment in a world where prices cannot decline because of market imperfections.

sources fully employed, the economy is capable of producing goods and services with a total value of $500 billion, while businesses produce only $400 billion worth of output, forces will be set into motion that tend to raise Y to the equilibrium level of $600 billion. As production expands, people and machines that were previously idle are put to work until Y reaches the full-employment level of $500 billion. With all resources fully employed, no further increase in output is possible, yet the forces driving Y toward $600 billion are still operating with full force. Something has to give, and that something is our assumption of a constant price level. At the full-employment level of $500 billion, there is an inflationary gap, and in fact aggregate demand exceeds aggregate supply by $50 billion. Y continues to increase above the full-employment level, but the increase consists entirely of an increase in prices, real output remaining constant. When Y reaches the equilibrium level of $600 billion, the inflation comes to an end.

III.   INCOME DETERMINATION BY MEANS OF THE CONSUMPTION FUNCTION: THE ALGEBRA

The geometric analysis we have just gone through is the traditional one. The results may also be derived by means of simple algebra. With all figures in billions of dollars, the consumption function depicted in Fig. 5–3 is

$$C = 100 + 0.5Y$$

With planned $I = 200$

$$\text{Aggregate demand} = C + I = 100 + 0.5Y + 200 = 300 + 0.5Y$$

$$\text{Aggregate supply} = Y$$

In equilibrium, therefore,

$$300 + 0.5Y = Y$$

and

$$Y = 600$$

When the full-employment level of Y $(Y_{fe}) = 500$,

$$\text{Aggregate demand} = 300 + 0.5 \times 500 = 550$$

There is an inflationary gap of $550 - 500 = 50$.

When $Y_{fe} = 800$, aggregate demand $= 300 + 0.5 \times 800 = 700$, resulting in a deflationary gap of $800 - 700 = 100$.

IV.   INCOME DETERMINATION BY MEANS OF THE SAVING FUNCTION: THE GEOMETRY

A third method may be used to derive the results of Section II. Figure 5-4, depicts the saving function corresponding to the consumption function of Fig. 5-3. Planned investment is independent of the level of income, the investment function is thus a horizontal line drawn through a vertical axis at 200. The equilibrium level of income is given by the intersection of the two functions—that is, at the level of Y where $S = I$: 600. It is readily seen that at full-employment levels of Y of 500 and 800 there are inflationary and deflationary gaps of 50 and 100, respectively.

V.   INCOME DETERMINATION BY MEANS OF THE SAVING FUNCTION: THE ALGEBRA

The saving function corresponding to the consumption function of Section III is

$$S = -100 + 0.5Y$$

With planned $I = 200$, the equality of S and I leads to

$$-100 + 0.5Y = 200$$

whence

$$Y = 600$$

When $Y_{fe} = 500$,

$$S = -100 + 0.5 \times 500 = 150$$

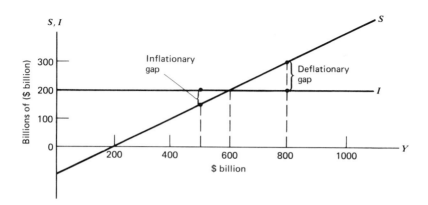

Figure 5-4. Income determination by means of the saving function.

Planned I exceeds saving by 50. Aggregate demand $(=C + I)$ therefore exceeds aggregate supply $(=C + S)$ by 50, there is an inflationary gap of that amount.

Further, when $Y_{fe} = 800$, $S = -100 + 0.5 \times 800 = 300$

Saving exceeds planned I by 100, the amount of the deflationary gap.

VI.   THE MULTIPLIER

Figure 5-5*a* shows the aggregate demand function we have already met in Fig. 5-3. There is no reason, of course, why planned investment should always be equal to $200 billion. In fact, investment tends to be very volatile, increasing as the economic skies lighten, declining as they become darker.

Suppose that in the following year the level of planned investment increases by $50 billion. To determine the new equilibrium level of Y (Y_e) we simply shift the aggregate demand function upward by that amount, and the intersection of the new function with the 45-degree line gives a new value of Y_e equal to $700 billion. Apparently, when I increases by $50 billion, Y increases by $100 billion.

Figure 5-5*b* depicts a different consumption function, and hence a different aggregate demand function. In this case when I increases by $50 billion, Y jumps from $600 billion to $850 billion, an increase of $250 billion.

The major difference between the two diagrams lies in the slope of the consumption function, the marginal propensity to consume. We must now examine the mechanism that turns an increase in I into a multiple increase in Y. Keynes called it the multiplier, and our preliminary investigation of the topic tells us that the marginal propensity to consume is one of its key components.

Let us begin by considering just one element of the increase in I: $10 million spent on the construction of a new factory. That $10 million represents profits to the owners of the construction firm that builds the factory and wages to the workers on the construction site. One further simplifying assumption is necessary: the income received in one time period is spent in the following time period.[3]

How much will be spent? That depends on the marginal propensity to consume. If it is 0.8, as it is in Fig. 5.5*b*, then $10 million received in time period 1 results in consumption of $(10 \times 0.8 = 8)$ million in time period 2.

---

3. Here a time period is not one year or one month, but the average length of time between the receipt of income and its expenditure.

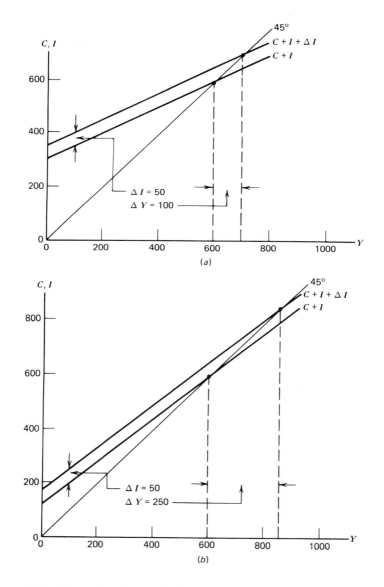

Figure 5-5. Introducing the multiplier.

Consumption for construction workers is income for other groups. Spending in supermarkets represents income for the owners and their employees. The new car purchase means additional income to the car dealer and the salespeople. The $8 million of extra income generated in time period 2 is spent in time period 3, resulting in consumption of $(8 × 0.8 = 6.4) million, which in turn generates $(6.4 × 0.8 = 5.12) million of additional income in time period 4. In theory the process continues indefinitely, but since the additional rounds of spending get smaller and smaller, after about ten or twelve time periods have elapsed, the process may be assumed to have run its course.

Consecutive rounds of consumption are also engendered by all of the other elements of the $50 billion increase in *I*. The aggregate process is shown diagrammatically in Fig. 5-6. Starting in equilibrium in time period 0, with GNP of $600 billion, the equilibrium is then disturbed by an increase in *I* of $50 billion in time period 1,

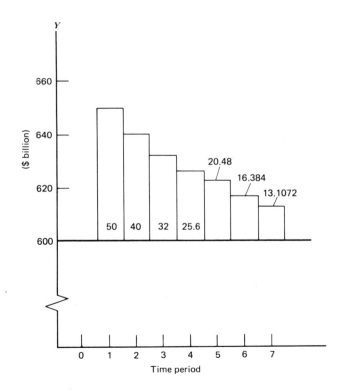

Figure 5-6. One-shot multiplier.

which leads to additional consumption in time period 2 of $(50 × 0.8 = 40) billion, $32 billion in time period 3, and so on. After ten or twelve time periods the economy has almost reestablished the old equilibrium level of $600 billion. In terms of Fig. 5-5, the aggregate demand function shifts up by $50 billion for one time period and then returns to the original position, where the equilibrium level of Y is the same as it was in the beginning. Since the increase in I occurs for one time period only, the multiplier involved is often referred to as the one-shot multiplier.

But the process depicted in Fig. 5-5 is somewhat different. It shows the aggregate demand function shifting upward and remaining there. In other words, the increase in I of $50 billion occurs not only in time period 1, but also in all succeeding time periods (see Fig. 5-7).

The starting point is the same as before: in time period 0 Y is in equilibrium at $600 billion, an equilibrium that is again disturbed by an increase in I of $50 billion. The increased investment in time period 1 leads to additional consumption in time period 2 of $40 billion. In time period 3 there will be further consumption of $40 billion resulting from the additional investment in time period 2, plus the consumption caused by the additional income generated by the extra consumption in time period 2. The pattern continues, with each increment of consumption getting larger, but by a smaller and smaller amount. The total increase in Y after a sufficient number of time periods has elapsed will be

$$\Delta Y = 50 + 40 + 32 + 25.6 + 20.48 + \ldots \tag{1}$$

which may be rewritten as

$$\Delta Y = 50(1 + 0.8 + 0.8^2 + 0.8^3 + \ldots) \tag{2}$$

Since there are an infinite number of terms (while each term gets closer and closer to zero, they never quite get there), it might appear at first that the sum is indeterminate. This is not so, and the sum may be determined by the following expedient (the technique is important, we will use it again). Multiply each side of the equality by 0.8.

$$0.8\Delta Y = 50(0.8 + 0.8^2 + 0.8^3 + 0.8^4 + \ldots) \tag{3}$$

Subtract Equation 3 from Equation 2.

$$\Delta Y - 0.8\Delta Y = 50(1) = 50 \tag{4}$$

This simple result follows because Equation 2 contains a 1 that does not appear in Equation 3. All the other terms in Equation 2

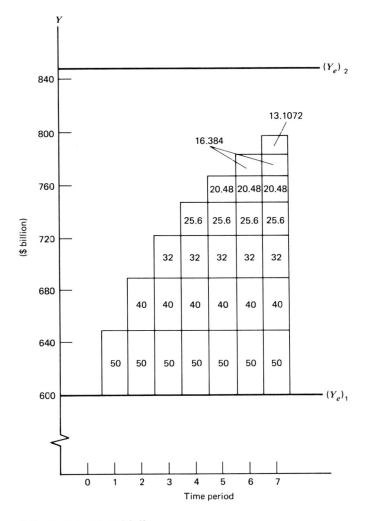

Figure 5-7. Sustained multiplier.

have an exact counterpart in Equation 3, so that when the latter is subtracted from the former they simply vanish, with the exception of the last term in Equation 3, which has no counterpart in Equation 2. But since each consecutive term gets smaller and smaller, that one must be infinitely small. In other words, it is equal to zero, and may be dropped. Continuing the manipulation,

$$0.2\Delta Y = 50 \qquad \Delta Y = 250$$

This result is the same one that we derived earlier by way of Fig. 5-5b. To distinguish it from the one-shot multiplier, the process just examined is known as the sustained multiplier.

Now let us look at the more general case, in which a sustained increase in investment equal to ΔI occurs in each time period, the marginal propensity to consume being c. Following the earlier pattern,

$$\Delta Y = \Delta I(1 + c + c^2 + c^3 + \ldots) \tag{5}$$

$$c\Delta Y = \Delta I(c + c^2 + c^3 + c^4 + \ldots) \tag{6}$$

Subtracting Equation 6 from Equation 5,

$$(1 - c)\Delta Y = \Delta I$$

whence

$$\frac{\Delta Y}{\Delta I} = \frac{1}{1 - c}$$

$\Delta Y/\Delta I$ is the investment multiplier and is indeed a function of the marginal propensity to consume as our earlier analysis predicted.

Recalling an earlier result from Chapter 4,

$$c + s = 1$$

s being the marginal propensity to save, it follows that

$$s = 1 - c$$

and hence that

$$\frac{\Delta Y}{\Delta I} = \frac{1}{s}$$

This formulation is perhaps easier to remember. The multiplier is simply the reciprocal of the marginal propensity to save.

To predict the effect on GNP of an increase in investment of $7 billion, the marginal propensity to consume being 0.75,

$$\frac{\Delta Y}{\Delta I} = \frac{1}{1 - c} = \frac{1}{1 - 0.75} = \frac{1}{0.25} = 4$$

$$\Delta Y = 4\Delta I = 4 \times 7 = \$28 \text{ billion}$$

Obviously other variables than investment affect the level of GNP. Strictly speaking, therefore, the investment multiplier tells us the effect on Y of a change in I, all other variables—except C—being held constant.[4]

Among the variables that affect the level of GNP are government spending and taxation. Since these are important policy variables, their impact will be discussed in the next chapter.

VII.   SUMMARY AND CONCLUSION

In this chapter several important links in the Keynesian chain were outlined.

1. The equality of saving and planned investment is brought about not by changes in the interest rate but by changes in the level of output, employment, and national income.
2. The economy tends toward a stable equilibrium that need not be the level of Y at which all resources are fully employed.
3. The multiplier process explains how a change in the level of planned investment leads to a multiple expansion (or contraction) in the GNP. The investment multiplier is equal to the reciprocal of the marginal propensity to save.

QUESTIONS

1. Given the aggregate consumption function

$$C = 2400 + 0.85Y$$

with all figures in billions of dollars, and planned investment equal to 300:
   (a) Calculate the equilibrium level of national income.
   (b) If the full-employment level of Y is 16,000, is there an inflationary or a deflationary gap? How large is it?
   (c) If Y_{fe} is 22,000, is there an inflationary or a deflationary gap? How large is it?
2. GNP is in equilibrium at $2200 billion. The equilibrium is then disturbed in time period 1 by a sustained increase in investment of $24 billion per time period. The MPC is 0.9. Calculate the level of GNP:
   (a) After two more time periods have elapsed;
   (b) After an infinite number of time periods have elapsed.

---

4. Readers with a background in calculus will recognize the multiplier as a partial derivative, which tells us the effect of a change in one variable on another, all other variables being held constant.

$$\frac{\delta Y}{\delta I} = \frac{1}{1 - c}$$

6 | Fiscal Policy

With the incorporation of a government sector, aggregate demand is made up of three components: consumption, investment, and government spending. In symbols,

$$Y = C + I + G$$

All the analysis of the preceding chapter is applicable, and the equilibrium level of income is determined by the intersection of aggregate demand and aggregate supply, $300 billion in Fig. 6−1. If Y_{fe} is $400 billion, there is a deflationary gap of $50 billion. An appropriate fiscal policy would be to increase G by that amount so that the intersection of the $C + I + G$ line and the 45 degree line occurs at the full-employment level of Y. If, on the other hand, Y_{fe} is $260 billion, there is an inflationary gap of $20 billion and an appropriate fiscal policy is to cut G by $20 billion.

Whether the vertical shift in the aggregate demand function is caused by a change in I, or by a change in G of equal magnitude, the change in Y will be the same, which means that the government spending multiplier is identical to the investment multiplier.

$$\frac{\Delta Y}{\Delta I} = \frac{1}{1 - C} \quad \text{Investment multiplier}$$

$$\frac{\Delta Y}{\Delta G} = \frac{1}{1 - C} \quad \text{Government spending multiplier}$$

The other side of the fiscal coin, taxation, affects aggregate demand through consumption. At first sight it might appear that a tax cut would have the same effect on aggregate demand as an equiva-

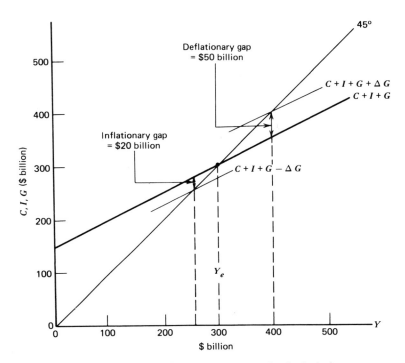

Figure 6-1. Determinants of GNP: government sector included.

lent increase in government spending. This is not so. A $1 billion increase in G represents spending of a like amount, but a $1 billion tax cut increases C by only that amount multiplied by the marginal propensity to consume. The rest of the tax cut is saved. Our third multiplier is therefore

$$\frac{\Delta Y}{\Delta T} = -\frac{C}{1-C} \quad \text{Tax multiplier}$$

The negative sign appears because a change in T causes a change in Y in the opposite direction. A tax cut (ΔT negative) causes Y to increase (ΔY positive); a tax increase (ΔT positive) results in a decline in Y (ΔY negative). These important results may also be derived algebraically.

I. A FISCAL MODEL

Economists often elaborate their theories in the form of a model. This is another word that does not have the same meaning as in everyday life. An economic model starts out by making certain assumptions, usually expressed in the form of a simultaneous equation system, which, when solved, results in statements about the key variables that can be subjected to testing by comparing the model to the real world. If the model survives such testing, it may be used to predict the values of those key variables, given the necessary data on other variables.

Some models are very complex indeed and consist of hundreds of simultaneous equations that can only be solved with the aid of a computer. Our model is very much simpler, consisting of only two equations

$$Y = C + I + G \qquad \text{Equality of aggregate supply and aggregate demand} \qquad (1)$$

$$C = C_0 + c(Y - T) \qquad \text{Consumption function} \qquad (2)$$

It will be observed that the consumption function is a little more complicated than it was when we had no government sector. Then we made the assumption (see the beginning of Chapter 4) that

$$Y = \text{NNP} = \text{NI} = \text{DPI}$$

While retaining the assumption of the equality of NNP and NI, for both of which we use the symbol Y, disposable personal income (DPI) is now equal to $Y - T$, and the new consumption function reflects the fact that consumption is a function of DPI. The system may be solved by substituting Equation 2 into Equation 1.

$$Y = C_0 + c(Y - T) + I + G$$

Multiplying out the bracket

$$Y = C_0 + cY - cT + I + G$$

Collecting the terms in Y together

$$Y - cY = C_0 - cT + I + G$$

Factor out the Y

$$(1 - c)Y = C_0 - cT + I + G$$

In equilibrium

$$Y = \frac{C_0 - cT + I + G}{1 - c} \qquad (3)$$

To calculate the government spending multiplier, increase G by an amount ΔG. This will cause Y to increase by an amount ΔY, where

$$Y + \Delta Y = \frac{C_0 - cT + I + G + \Delta G}{1 - c}$$

Separate the ΔG term from the other terms on the right-hand side

$$Y + \Delta Y = \frac{C_0 - cT + I + G}{1 - c} + \frac{\Delta G}{1 - c}$$

The first term on the right-hand side is equal to Y; we have just shown that in Equation 3. It and the Y on the left therefore cancel each other out, leaving

$$\Delta Y = \frac{\Delta G}{1 - c}$$

or

$$\frac{\Delta Y}{\Delta G} = \frac{1}{1 - c}$$

The tax multiplier may be derived in similar fashion.[1]

$$Y + \Delta Y = \frac{C_0 - c(T + \Delta T) + I + G}{1 - c}$$

Multiply out the bracket

$$Y + \Delta Y = \frac{C_0 - cT - c\Delta T + I + G}{1 - c}$$

$$Y + \Delta Y = \frac{C_0 - cT + I + G}{1 - c} - \frac{c\Delta T}{1 - c}$$

Subtract Y from each side

$$\Delta Y = - \frac{c\Delta T}{1 - c} \qquad\qquad \frac{\Delta Y}{\Delta T} = - \frac{c}{1 - c}$$

In this section we have looked at the effect on Y when either G or T is changed. What happens when both G and T are free to change? One possibility is discussed in the next section.

II.   THE CONSERVATIVE'S DILEMMA

The word *conservative* has many connotations. In the economic sphere one thinks of someone who believes in two major principles: "small government" and "balanced budgets."

---

1. A knowledge of partial derivatives enables us to derive directly from Equation 3.

$$\frac{\delta Y}{\delta G} = \frac{1}{1 - c}; \qquad \frac{\delta Y}{\delta T} = - \frac{c}{1 - c}$$

Can the use of fiscal policy be consistent with these two tenets? First thoughts are that the answer is no. If we start with a budget in balance, that is, with $G = T$, then a tax cut, or an increase in government spending, will result in a budget deficit, which is inconsistent with the second conservative precept. If we recall, however, that the government spending multiplier is larger than the tax multiplier, second thoughts might suggest that the use of fiscal policy and a belief in balanced budgets can be consistent.

Suppose we start with a balanced budget, increase government spending by an amount ΔG, and increase taxes by ΔT so that $\Delta G = \Delta T$. Clearly the budget is still balanced. The net effect of this double-barreled policy on GNP will be an increase of

$$\Delta Y = \frac{1}{1 - c} \Delta G - \frac{c}{1 - c} \Delta T$$

Since $\Delta G = \Delta T$, this may be rewritten as

$$\Delta Y = \frac{1}{1 - c} \Delta G - \frac{c}{1 - c} \Delta G = \left[\frac{1}{1 - c} - \frac{c}{1 - c}\right] \Delta G$$

Putting the right-hand side over its common denominator $1 - c$

$$\Delta Y = \left[\frac{1 - c}{1 - c}\right] \Delta G = \Delta G$$

whence

$$\frac{\Delta Y}{\Delta G} = 1$$

In economic terms the government collected income in the form of taxes, only part of which was being spent, and spends all of it.

The expression just derived is called the "balanced budget multiplier." It is completely independent of the marginal propensity to consume—that canceled out in the last step but one—and is, in fact, identically equal to unity. But another way, an equal increase in G and T will result in an increase in Y of the same amount.

$$\Delta G = \Delta T = \Delta Y$$

Balanced budgets and fiscal policy are consistent. A problem now arises with the other conservative tenet: "small government."

Suppose that, to reduce unemployment, we want to increase GNP by $20 billion. Suppose further than the marginal propensity to consume is 0.8. What options do we have? First we need to calculate the multipliers.

$$\frac{\Delta Y}{\Delta G} = \frac{1}{1 - c} = \frac{1}{1 - 0.8} = \frac{1}{0.2} = 5$$

$$\frac{\Delta Y}{\Delta T} = -\frac{c}{1 - c} = -\frac{0.8}{1 - 0.8} = -\frac{0.8}{0.2} = -4$$

The balanced budget multiplier is always

$$\frac{\Delta Y}{\Delta G} = 1$$

We have a choice of three policies:

1. Increase government spending by $(20/5 = 4) billion.
2. Cut taxes by $(20/4 = 5) billion.
3. Increase both G and T by $20 billion.

Here, then, is the conservative's dilemma. The first two policies result in an unbalanced budget; the third requires a much larger increase in both government spending and taxes—in the share of GNP going to the government sector.[2] Most economic conservatives surmount the dilemma by rejecting fiscal policy as a means of manipulating the economy.

III.   TAXES AS A FUNCTION OF INCOME

While our model has introduced a government sector, and thus represents an advance over the simpler analysis of Chapter 5, it does not go far enough. Taxes are not set by government; tax rates are. Although they can make educated guesses, fiscal planners do not know in advance what tax receipts will be. That depends on the level of national income, and our next model reflects this fact. Taxes are shown explicitly as a (linear) function of income.

$$Y = C + I + G \tag{4}$$

$$C = C_0 + c(Y - T) \tag{5}$$

$$T = T_0 + tY \tag{6}$$

---

2. If the goal is to reduce inflation, a conservative can have the best of both worlds. An equal reduction in G and T will keep the budget in balance, and the reduction in the size of the government sector will be greater than with a decline in G, which is not offset. For reasons discussed in Chapter 9, however, fiscal policy has been used far more often to reduce unemployment than to cure inflation.

The coefficient of Y in the third equation, t, may be thought of as the marginal propensity to tax, but is more commonly referred to as the marginal tax rate. To obtain the equilibrium level of Y, substitute Equation 6 in Equation 5.

$$C = C_0 + C(Y - T_0 - tY) = C_0 + cY - cT_0 - ctY \tag{7}$$

Now substitute Equation 7 in Equation 4.

$$Y = C_0 + cY - cT_0 - ctY + I + G$$

Collect the terms in Y on the left

$$Y - cY + ctY = C_0 - cT_0 + I + G$$

Factor out the Y

$$(1 - c + ct)Y = c_0 - cT_0 + I + G$$

Whence

$$Y = \frac{C_0 - cT_0 + I + G}{1 - c + ct}$$

The multipliers may be calculated using the same approach as before. They are, respectively,

$$\frac{\Delta Y}{\Delta I} = \frac{1}{1 - c + ct} \quad \text{The Investment multiplier}$$

$$\frac{\Delta Y}{\Delta G} = \frac{1}{1 - c + ct} \quad \text{The Government spending multiplier}$$

$$\frac{\Delta Y}{\Delta T_0} = \frac{c}{1 - c + ct} \quad \text{The Tax multiplier}$$

If the denominators of the multipliers are written, as they can be, as $1 - c(1 - t)$, the economic logic becomes clear. Of an extra dollar of income, $\$t$ will be taken in taxes, leaving $\$(1 - t)$ available for spending. The amount actually spent will therefore be $\$c(1 - t)$, and that term fulfills the same role as c in the simpler model examined earlier.

The tax multiplier shows the effect of a change in the portion of taxes that is independent of income. The effect of a change in the marginal tax rate is more complicated and will not be derived here. For the sake of completeness, however, it is

$$\frac{\Delta Y}{\Delta t} = -\frac{cY}{1 - c + ct}$$

IV.   THE MULTIPLIERS COMPARED

It is instructive to compare these multipliers with those derived from the first model, in which taxes were independent of income. Suppose that the marginal propensity to consume is 0.8 as before, and the marginal tax rate, t, is 0.25.

$$\frac{\Delta Y}{\Delta G} = \frac{1}{1 - c + ct} = \frac{1}{1 - 0.8 + 0.8 \times 0.25}$$

$$= \frac{1}{1 - 0.8 + 0.2} = \frac{1}{0.4} = 2.5$$

The multiplier is smaller—2.5 versus 5.0 when taxes are independent of income. The difference is due to the fact that, when taxes are independent of income, an increase in G (an injection) causes saving (a leakage) to increase with income until, in equilibrium, the increased saving exactly matches the increase in G. With a marginal propensity to consume of 0.8, the marginal propensity to save is 0.2. An increase of G of \$4 billion causes an increase in Y of \$20 billion, which means an increase in saving of \$(20 × 0.2 = 4) billion.

When taxes are a function of income, two leakages increase. If the multiplier is 2.5, an increase in G of \$4 billion results in an increase in Y of \$10 billion. This, in turn, causes taxes to increase by \$(10 × 0.25 = 2.5) billion, meaning that disposable income increases by \$(10 − 2.5 = 7.5) billion, and hence saving by \$(7.5 × 0.2 = 1.5) billion. Leakages increase by a total of \$(2.5 + 1.5 = 4) billion, the same as the increase in G.

It might seem too bad that in the real world taxes increase with income—the multiplier effect is smaller. While this is true, the effect on the budget deficit is also smaller. Suppose we start with a budget in balance and want to increase Y by \$20 billion. In the model with a multiplier of 5.0, the needed increase in G is \$4 billion, and the budget moves into deficit by that amount. When the multiplier is only 2.5, the increase in G needs to be \$8 billion, but this is offset by increased taxes equal to \$(20 × 0.25 = 5) billion. The deficit is only \$3 billion.

V.   CAN A TAX CUT STIMULATE THE ECONOMY WITHOUT INCREASING THE DEFICIT?

Some economists—and some politicians too—argue that a cut in the marginal tax rate, t will actually result in an increase in taxes, T, because of the stimulative effect on the economy. Let us examine this proposition in terms of our model. Suppose that

$$Y = C + I + G$$
$$C = 100 + 0.8(Y - T)$$
$$T = 225 + 0.25Y$$
$$I = 125$$
$$G = 675$$

All figures are in billions of dollars. Noting that $C_0 = 100$, $c = 0.8$, $T_0 = 225$, and $t = 0.25$, the equilibrium level of Y will be

$$Y = \frac{C_0 - cT_0 + I + G}{1 - c + ct} = \frac{100 - 0.8 \times 225 + 125 + 675}{1 - 0.8 + 0.8 \times 0.25}$$

$$= \frac{900 - 180}{0.4} = 1800$$

$$T = T_0 + tY = 225 + 0.25 \times 1800 = 225 + 450 = 675$$

The budget is balanced: $G = T = 675$.

Suppose that the marginal tax rate is cut to 0.2, all the other variables remaining the same. GNP will increase to

$$Y = \frac{C_0 - cT_0 + I + G}{1 - c + ct} = \frac{720}{1 - 0.8 + 0.8 \times 0.2}$$

$$= \frac{720}{0.36}$$

$$= 2000$$

Now let us see what happens to taxes.

$$T = T_0 + tY = 225 + 0.2 \times 2{,}000 = 225 + 400 = 625$$

Tax receipts have declined by \$50 billion, and the budget is now in deficit by that amount. Apparently the proposition is incorrect, and so it is by the assumptions of our model. Proponents would criticize those assumptions, however, pointing to the effect of the cut in the marginal tax rate on incentives. (For a more detailed discussion of this viewpoint, see Section VII of this chapter and Chapter 12.) With more of their pretax income going into their pockets, workers might worker harder for longer hours. Businesses might expand production and investment. This is an issue that cannot be settled by analysis alone, and certainly not in terms of the simple models we have been using.

VI. THE PARADOX OF THRIFT

The time has come to examine another simplifying assumption in our models: that investment is equal to whatever business people in the aggregate decide it should be. This assumption results in investment being independent of the level of GNP, or, to say the same thing in a different fashion, the investment function is parallel to the Y-axis. Isn't it more likely to be the case that as GNP increases, investment increases also? Such an assumption has some interesting implications. Figure 6-2 illustrates one of them. The equilibrium level of Y is determined by the intersection of the saving function (S_1) and the investment function (I): Y_e = \$500 billion. At that level of Y

$$S = I = \$150 \text{ billion.}$$

Now suppose for some reason that the household sector decides to save more. That behavioral assumption is shown by the upward shift in the saving function to S_2. Y_e declines from \$500 billion to \$250 billion, where

$$S = I = \$100 \text{ billion}$$

Here, then, is a paradox—the "paradox of thrift." When everyone tries to save more, all end up saving less.

The paradox is resolved by thinking a little more rigorously about the meaning of the phrase *save more*. Since the shift in the saving function is a parallel shift, the marginal propensity to save has not

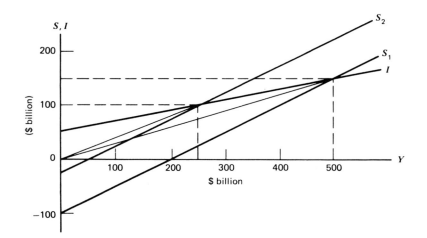

Figure 6-2. Paradox of thrift.

changed; the average propensity has increased.[3] At $Y_e = 500$ the APS
is

$$\frac{S}{Y} = \frac{150}{500} = 0.3$$

whereas at $Y_e = 250$ it is

$$\frac{S}{Y} = \frac{100}{250} = 0.4$$

The household sector is saving a larger fraction of a smaller income.

VII.   THE SUPERMULTIPLIER

The assumption that investment is a function of GNP can be incor-
porated into our model. For the sake of simplicity we revert to the
formulation of Chapter 5, in which there was no government sector.
The model thus becomes

$$Y = C + I \tag{8}$$

$$C = C_0 + cY \tag{9}$$

$$I = I_0 + fY \tag{10}$$

We cannot use i as the coefficient of Y in the third equation. That
traditionally serves as the symbol for the rate of interest. I_0, the
component of investment that is independent of Y, is known as
autonomous investment; fY, the component that does vary with Y,
is induced investment. Following our earlier terminology, f may be
thought of as the marginal propensity to invest. The model is solved
by substituting Equations 9 and 10 into Equation 8, which leads to

$$Y = C_0 + cY + I_0 + fY$$

Collecting the terms in Y on the left and factoring,

$$(1 - c - f)Y = C_0 + I_0$$

The equilibrium level of Y is

$$Y = \frac{C_0 + I_0}{1 - c - f}$$

---

3. Recall that the APS is represented geometrically by the slope of a line from the origin to the
relevant point on the saving function.

Or, recalling that $1 - c = s$,

$$Y = \frac{C_0 + I_0}{s - f}$$

The investment multiplier may be derived in the usual way.

$$\frac{\Delta Y}{\Delta I_0} = \frac{1}{s - f}$$

Since f is positive, it follows that $s - f < s$, and therefore that

$$\frac{1}{s - f} > \frac{1}{s}$$

$1/s$ is the multiplier when investment is independent of Y. The one just derived is greater—hence the name "supermultiplier." For example, if the marginal propensity to save is 0.2 and investment is independent of Y (the marginal propensity to invest is zero), the investment multiplier is

$$\frac{\Delta Y}{\Delta I} = \frac{1}{s} = \frac{1}{0.2} = 5.0$$

If the marginal propensity to invest is 0.1, the multiplier becomes

$$\frac{\Delta Y}{\Delta I_0} = \frac{1}{s - f} = \frac{1}{0.2 - 0.1} = \frac{1}{0.1} = 10.0$$

An increase in autonomous investment results in a tenfold increase in Y.

Here is perhaps one reason why tax cuts may be more potent than our earlier analysis indicated. Part of an increase in income not spent by consumers is now spent by the business sector. Not only does consumption expand as a result of a tax cut, investment does, too.

VIII.   AUTOMATIC STABILIZERS

We began our analysis by assuming a state of anarchy: no government sector at all. Next we introduced a government sector and examined the consequences of its undertaking certain fiscal policies. There is an interesting in-between state of affairs in which there is a government sector, but it is inactive in the sense that it does not continually change its policies. It decides on a level of government spending, on a tax structure, and on a system of transfer payments, but then leaves them unchanged, no matter what the economy may be doing. Is an inactive government sector equivalent to no government sector at all? It is not.

Suppose that in Fig. 6–3, in the absence of a government sector, the economy follows the path shown by the thick black line labeled *NG* (no government). With a government sector, as GNP rises from *A* to *B*, output and incomes increase, and more workers are employed. As the economy approaches the full-employment level, prices begin to rise, and the economic malaise of the day is inflation.

With a progressive income tax, the recipients of higher incomes move into higher tax brackets and taxes increase. As more and more people find jobs, government payments to the unemployed decline and transfer payments decrease. Both forms of medicine are appropriate treatments for the disorder. As a result of their application GNP actually traces the path *AE* along the thin line labeled *WG* (with government).

When the economy moves into a recession, so that in a state of anarchy it would trace the path *BC*, output and incomes decline and workers are laid off. Lower incomes mean lower tax brackets: taxes decline. A higher rate of unemployment means that government payments to the unemployed are stepped up; transfer payments increase. These remedies are helpful when the malady is recession and unemployment; their effect is to move the economy along the path *EF*.

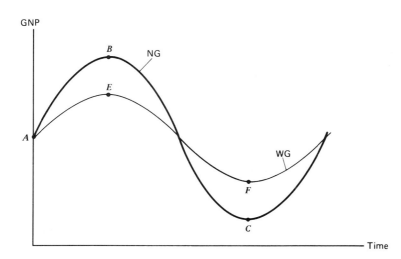

Figure 6-3. Automatic stabilizers.

Because these mechanisms work to stabilize the economy—they make the swings in GNP narrower than they would otherwise be, in much the same way that an automatic pilot prevents an aircraft from straying too far from its course, even without the pilot's hands on the controls—they are known as automatic stabilizers. The two most important automatic stabilizers are the progressive income tax, as well as other taxes that depend on the level of economic activity, and the system of transfer payments to the unemployed. They do not eliminate boom and bust—positive government actions are still needed for that—but they do moderate their excesses.

In recent years the United States economy has become subject to a destabilizing influence, an automatic destabilizer if you like. Many labor contracts contain COLAs—the cost of living adjustments—that automatically increase wages by a higher amount in times of rapid inflation, and by a lower amount in periods when prices are rising less rapidly. COLAs increase purchasing power, hence consumption and aggregate demand, in inflationary periods, while doing the reverse in recessions, the exact opposite of what is needed for stability.

The topic is controversial. Some economists emphasize the destabilizing effects of COLAs, while others claims that their existence leads to wage demands being more moderate because workers have an automatic source of protection in periods of inflation.

What cannot be disputed is that the presence of COLAs causes the effects of external shocks—a large rise in oil prices by the OPEC cartel, for example—to be much more serious than would be the case in their absence. Instead of affecting only industries in which oil is a major input, an OPEC price increase, through the medium of COLAs, also increases labor costs in many other industries, magnifying the inflationary impact of the external shock.

IX. BUDGET POLICIES

In the short run those responsible for the nation's budget policies have to consider two major questions: (1) what degree of fiscal stimulus or restraint is needed and (2) what fraction of the nation's resources should go to the government sector?

The answers to these questions need not be inconsistent. To apply stimulus and increase the size of the government sector, an increase in government spending is appropriate, whereas if stimulus is needed together with a reduction in the government take, a tax cut will do the trick.

Over the longer run those responsible for decisions have a variety of choices with regard to whether or not the budget is to be balanced, and at what intervals. In this regard there are four main choices.

A. Balance the Budget Every Year

Following the success of Proposition 13 in California, which rolled back state taxes, some groups are pushing a constitutional amendment that would require the federal government to balance its budget in each and every year. Such a goal would be difficult to achieve and would be destabilizing.

The discussion earlier in this chapter pointed up the fact that the federal government sets tax rates for taxes. Actual tax revenues depend on the level of national income. When that is high, revenues will be higher than when it is low, even with identical tax rates. There is thus a forecasting problem, and economists' track records in this department are not very encouraging.

Furthermore, the requirement for a balanced budget means that the automatic stabilizers have to be offset. In times of inflation, when the budget tends to move into surplus, taxes must be cut and/or government spending increased, meausres that tend to make the inflation even worse. Conversely, when recession causes a budget deficit, tax increases and spending cuts designed to eliminate the deficit cannot help but make the recession worse. To get around the problems associated with annually balanced budgets, some economists advocate a second course.

B. Balance the Budget Over the Course of the Business Cycle

The use of fiscal policy to iron the ups and downs of the business cycle requires budget deficits in times of recession, surpluses in inflationary periods. If each deficit is exactly offset by a subsequent surplus, the national debt need neither increase nor decrease. The problem with this seemingly ideal budget policy is that the right amount of fiscal stimulus needed in a recession might not match the amount of restraint appropriate for the ensuing upswing. This policy therefore ties the hands of policymakers somewhat, although it does not make the cycles worse as does the annually balanced budget. If policymakers' hands are to be completely free, the appropriate budgetary policy is functional finance.

C. Functional Finance

Proponents of functional finance argue that fiscal policy should be determined by the needs of stabilization policy alone and not by the effect of such policies on the national debt. If the end result is a larger, or a smaller, national debt, so be it. Unfortunately, given government's prediliction to cut taxes and increase spending, along with its aversion to do the opposite, an increasing national debt can almost be guaranteed when all restraints are removed. One small surplus and nineteen deficits in the last twenty years, with the national debt growing from $383 billion in fiscal 1970 to $900 billion in 1980,[4] represent the kind of results that may be expected from this version of freewheeling fiscal policy. To introduce a modicum of discipline into the nation's finances, economists look at another concept.

D. The Full-Employment Budget

Since the level of national income cannot be predicted with any degree of accuracy, why not simply assume some value for national income, say that associated with 4 percent unemployment rate, and set tax rates to balance the budget at that level? If the unemployment rate is higher, say 6 percent, national income and hence tax receipts will be lower than at the percent level, and the budget moves into deficit, precisely the right move to reduce unemployment. On the other hand, if the unemployment rate is only 3 percent, inflation is almost certain to be the problem of the day, tax receipts will be higher, and the budget is surplus, just the right remedy for incipient inflation.

While seemingly a step in the right direction, the full-employment budget concept has been misused. Even when running back-to-back deficits of $23 billion in each of fiscal years 1971 and 1972, President Nixon was able to claim that the full-employment budget was close to balance in each year. Economists should never underestimate the ability of politicians to turn their latest theories to political advantage in ways that cannot be foreseen.

X.   THE EQUALITY OF SAVING AND INVESTMENT WITH A GOVERNMENT SECTOR

With the introduction of a government sector, NNP is made up of consumption spending, net investment, and government spending. National income is either consumed, saved, or taxed. In symbols,

$$Y = C + I + G \qquad Y = C + S + T$$

$$\text{(NNP)} \qquad\qquad \text{(NI)}$$

In equilibrium, therefore,

$$C + I + G = C + S + T$$

Subtracting C from each side and rearranging,

$$S + T = I + G$$

---

4. Estimated. Source: *Economic Report of the President*, 1979, pp. 264–265.

In terms of Fig. 2–5, this formulation simply states that for a constant circular flow the sum of the two leakages $(S + T)$ must be equal to the sum of the two injections $(I + G)$.

In the absence of a government sector, the equilibrium condition, developed in Chapter 5, was:

$$S = I$$

where I was defined as planned investment, and was in fact equal to realized investment in equilibrium.

These two results may be shown to be equivalent by the following simple expedient:

$$S + T = I + G$$

Rearranging,

$$S + (T - G) = I$$

The term in parenthesis is equal to government receipts minus government expenditures; in other words, it represents government saving. The equality of saving and investment still holds, even with the introduction of a government sector, if saving is defined to include government saving, $T - G$. Should government spending happen to exceed tax receipts, as it will if the budget is in deficit, government saving will be negative, but the equality still holds. This result will make life very much simpler for us when a more sophisticated level of analysis is introduced in Chapter 9.

XI. FISCAL POLICY IN ACTION

Fiscal policy had its greatest success in 1964. President John F. Kennedy tried for two years to push a tax cut through the Congress but failed. After Kennedy was assassinated in November 1963, Lyndon Johnson became president, and in the honeymoon period that followed his inauguration, succeeded in getting the tax cut through. The result was all that economists had predicted. Unemployment declined from 5.7 percent in 1963 to 3.8 percent in 1966. These gains were not achieved at the expense of a rapidly rising price level. Inflation, as measured by the consumer price index, rose from 1.2 percent in 1963 to 1.7 percent in 1965, and was still only 2.9 percent in 1966. In this period Keynesians were riding high, and the precepts of *The General Theory* attained their greatest level of acceptance.

From then on it was all downhill. Johnson's tax surcharge in 1968, designed to choke off a rising rate of inflation, was a failure. The inflation rate of 6.1 percent in 1969 was the highest in twenty years.

In the 1970s we witnessed a federal budget seemingly out of control. The 1975 deficit of $45 billion was incurred in a year when the inflation rate was 9.1 percent. The record deficit of $66 billion in 1976 exceeded even the massive deficits of World War II, and coexisted with an inflation rate of 5.8 percent. True, these deficits succeeded in reducing 1975's unemployment rate of 8.5 to 6.0 percent in 1978, but a rising price level with massive amounts of excess capacity is situation about which *The General Theory* is silent.

As these lines were written, in the fifth year of an economic expansion, the federal government is projecting a deficit for fiscal 1980 of $29 billion.[5] There is talk of budget stringency in the future, but whether talk will be translated into action, only time will tell.

XII.   SUMMARY AND CONCLUSION

Fiscal policy affects the level of economic activity through changes in government spending and taxes. Because the tax multiplier is smaller, in absolute value, than the government-spending multiplier, the balanced-budget multiplier is positive and equal to one.

When taxes are a function of income, the mulpliers are smaller. Under the assumptions of the Keynesian model, a cut in tax rate will stimulate the economy, but not sufficiently to restore taxes to their original level.

When investment is a function of income, the multipliers are larger, but we are faced with the paradox of thrift—when we all try to save more, we end up saving less.

Automatic stabilizers tend to keep the economy on course, but in recent years a destabilizing influence has appeared in the form of cost of living adjustments.

An attempt to balance the budget in each and every year would be destabilizing through its effect in offsetting the automatic stabilizers. Other forms of budget policy are stabilizing.

The budget deficits of recent years cannot be blamed on Keynesian economic policies, which would require budget surpluses in periods of inflation, but have instead resulted from a lack of discipline on the part of those responsible for the conduct of fiscal policy.

QUESTIONS

1. If taxes are not a function of income and the MPC is 0.75, $Y_e = 1600$ billion and $Y_{fe} = \$1648$ billion:
   (a)   Calculate the government-spending multiplier.

---

5. Source for all data in this section: *Economic Report of the President*, 1979, pp. 217, 244, 264, and 265.

(b) Calculate the tax multiplier.
(c) Calculate the balanced-budget multiplier.
(d) Suggest three suitable fiscal policies based on your answers to (a), (b), and (c).
2. Given the model

$$Y = C + I + G$$

$$C = C_0 + c(Y - T)$$

$$T = T_0 + tY$$

an MPC of 0.8, a marginal tax rate of 6.25 percent, and a budget deficit of $10 billion:
(a) Calculate the government-spending multiplier.
(b) Suggest a suitable fiscal policy based on (a) if Y_e and Y_{fe} are the same as in Question 1.
(c) What will the new budget deficit (or surplus) be once the full effects of your proposed policy have worked themselves out?
3. Given the aggregate saving and investment functions:

$$S = -1500 + 0.25Y$$

$$I = 900 + 0.05Y$$

(a) Calculate the equilibrium value of Y.
(b) Calculate the value of S when $Y = Y_e$.
(c) Calculate the APS when $Y = Y_e$.

Now suppose that everyone tries to save more so that the aggregate saving function becomes

$$S = -1500 + 0.3Y$$

(d) Illustrate the paradox of thrift.
(e) Resolve it.
(f) How does this case differ from the one we discussed in the text?

7 | Money and Monetary Policy

What is humanity's most significant invention? Fire? The steam engine? The assembly line? Electricity? The blast furnance? Railways? The automobile? Clearly all were extremely important and changed our mode of life in far-reaching ways. Yet perhaps the most significant of all is not included in the preceding list. The title of the chapter gives it away: money.

Think of what life would be like in a society with no acceptable form of money. Goods would have to be exchanged for goods instead of being bought and sold with money. The economic term for this is *barter*. In a barter economy the hungry shoemaker cannot spend every minute making footwear. The shoemaker must track down a baker who needs a pair of shoes. The candlestickmaker whose wife expresses a wish for a new gown must hope that sooner or later he will meet a dressmaker with a yen for candlesticks. Life would be extremely frustrating and living standards very low.

It is true that in such a society specialists soon appear on the scene, people devoting their lives to bringing together the baker and the makers of candlesticks, dresses, and shoes. Such specialists might even engineer complex exchanges in which the baker with worn-out shoes gives a loaf to a hungry dressmaker, who clothes the wife of a candlestickmaker, who manufactures a candlestick for the shoemaker, who completes the transaction by cobbling a new pair of shoes for the baker. These specialists, or brokers, are not unknown in the twentieth century when a country's currency is in ill repute. They had their heyday in the Germany of the 1930s, when they arranged trades of aspirin for Brazilian coffee, mouth organs for

Rumanian oil, and steel from the valley of the Ruhr for Chilean copper and nitrates.

The existence of an acceptable form of money makes life much simpler. The baker exchanges bread for money, which is used to purchase shoes, candlesticks, clothes or whatever else may seem necessary. Used in such a manner, money is a medium of exchange. It enables the baker to spend time using a skill: baking bread. Money increases efficiency and hence output and living standards. For this reason some economists even go so far as to classify money as one of the factors of production, along with land, labor, and capital.

The baker may also bury the money in a tin box at the foot of the garden, to be dug up in the future as a dowry for a daughter, or to pay the passage for a child seeking a new life in another country. Money can thus also be a store of value.

GNP in the United States in 1978 was $2107 billion. Here GNP is expressed in dollars, reflecting money's third role as a unit of account. When debts are denominated in dollars, money serves as a standard of deferred payment.

I. MONEY DEFINED

What is money? The reader will automatically think of the dollar bill in a wallet or purse, or the quarter and the dime nestled together in a pocket. All of these are money, but the term has a much broader compass. Many things have served as money, and the only important criterion is that they be so accepted. Some American Indian tribes of two centurie ago used wampum—polished shells strung together to form a belt or sash. Early African explorers took along coils of copper wire with which to purchase necessary supplies from the tribes through whose territories they passed. In the era of the slave trade in Ethiopia, a sack of salt would purchase a slave, and even today some African men pay for their brides with cattle.

For hundreds of years in Europe money meant gold and silver coins, or paper money that could be exchanged for them on demand. Only monarchs had the right to mint coins, and when they found the expense of a foreign war, or of a new palace, exceeding the funds available, they sometimes alloyed the gold or silver with base metals to make them go further. Therein lies the origin of the phrase *to debase the currency.*

In the United States of today money is defined in a variety of ways because economists cannot agree on what should be called money and what should not be. The problem is where to draw the line between money and money substitutes known as near-monies.

Everyone's definition would include coin and currency, the first made of a variety of metals, the second including dollars bills and other forms of paper. These may be used to make any purchase, accepted anywhere in the United States and sometimes in other countries too. A checking account enables the owner of the checkbook to make a payment by writing a check. There may be problems with out-of-town checks, and sometimes a driver's license or other form of identification must be produced, but a check receives widespread acceptance, and hence deposits in checking accounts are included in all economists' definition of money. Because money deposited in a checking account may be withdrawn on demand, the economist's term for such an account is a *demand deposit*. A widely accepted definition of the money stock, for which the symbol M_1 is used, is

$$M_1 = \text{Currency (including coin)} + \text{Demand deposits}$$

"Near money" is something that is not money, but is readily convertible into money. For example, a deposit in a savings account at a commercial bank may quickly be withdrawn—converted into money. If you read the small print in your savings book, you will find that the bank has the right to require one-month's notice before you make a withdrawal. This is a right that banks never enforce. If they tried to do so they would rapidly find their accounts fleeing elsewhere. But, because at least theoretically, time must elapse beteen the request for a withdrawal and the withdrawal itself, these deposits are known as "time deposits." Another common definition of the money stock is

$$M_2 = M_1 + \text{Time deposits at commercial banks}$$

Other definitions of money, labeled M_3, M_4, etc., include other forms of near-monies: deposits at saving and loan institutions, treasury bills, and so on. For our purposes, however, a knowledge of M_1 and M_2 will suffice.

In December 1978, the United States money stock (M_1) stood at $361.1 billion, made up of $97.5 billion in currency and $263.6 billion in demand deposits. M_2 was equal to $872.0 billion.[1]

II.   THE QUANTITY EQUATION OF EXCHANGE

Think for a moment of the nickel or dime you have in your pocket. That coin has undoubtedly traveled widely during the past year, from supermarket till to homemaker's purse, to slot machine, to

---

1. Source: *Economic Report of the President*, 1979, p. 251.

bank, to traveling salesperson's pocket, to a waiter in the form of a tip. A five-dollar bill, if you have one, has also traveled from place to place in the same time period, but probably not so rapidly, and a hundred-dollar bill would change hands even less frequently. Nevertheless, it is possible to think in terms of the average number of times that the stock of money turns over, or changes hands, in one year. Economists call it the "velocity of circulation," or "velcocity" for short.

In 1978 GNP was equal to $2106.6 billion. This figure does not strictly reflect the total volume of financial transactions in that year because, it will be recalled, the GNP does not include the sale of secondhand goods and some other transactions of a similar nature. Nevertheless it does serve as a useful approximation, and enables us to calculate the velocity of circulation for that year. In 1978, a total of $352.8 billion[2] of money facilitated transactions of approximately $2106.6 billion. Velocity was therefore

$$V = \frac{\$2106.6}{\$352.8} = 5.97$$

More generally, velocity may be calculated as follows:

$$V = \frac{GNP}{M}$$

where M = money stock.

Since GNP is made up of a real component and a price component (see Chapter 2),

$$GNP = PQ$$

where P = price component and Q real output.

$$V = \frac{GNP}{M} = \frac{PQ}{M}$$

Multiplying each side of the equation by M,

$$MV = PQ$$

This formulation is known as the quantity equation of exchange. Simple as it is, it gives us some useful insights into economic phenomena and serves to introduce the topic of monetary policy.

---

2. The figure ($M1$) for June 1978, is close to the average for the year. Source: *Economic Report of the President,* 1979, pp. 183 and 231.

A. What Causes Inflation?

V, the velocity of circulation, stays relatively constant in the short run. It is said to be "stable." It depends on institutional factors—how often workers get paid: weekly, monthly, or whatever—and these things change slowly. Suppose that the economy is at full employment. Real output (Q) cannot increase. What happens when M is increased? For the equality to hold, P must increase.

$$\begin{array}{ccccc} & \uparrow & & \uparrow & \text{Cannot increase above} \\ \text{Constant} & M\ V & = & P\ Q & \text{full-employment level} \\ & \underline{\qquad\qquad} & & \underline{\qquad\qquad} & \end{array}$$

The quantity equation of exchange has given us a simple explanation for inflation—that is, a sustained rise in P. During the 300 years after 1500, the price level in Europe rose steadily and continuously as gold and silver flowed in from the mines in the New World. In those days gold and money were equivalent and the rise in prices was linked directly to the increase in the money supply.

B. Monetary Policy

Since inflation is caused by a too rapid growth in the money supply, an appropriate monetary policy would appear to be to decrease the money supply, or because this would be drastic medicine, to slow its rate of growth.

$$\begin{array}{cc} \downarrow & \downarrow \\ M\ V & = P\ Q \end{array}$$

Unfortunately, this policy has an undesirable side effect. While Q cannot increase above the full-employment level, there is nothing to stop it from decreasing. When wages and prices are sticky in a downward direction, a decrease in output and an increase in unemployment accompany the slowdown in inflation.

$$\begin{array}{cc} \downarrow & \downarrow\ \downarrow \\ M\ V & = P\ Q \end{array}$$

Conversely, when monetary policy is used to fight unemployment, a side effect is an increase in the rate of inflation. The appropriate policy is an increase in the money supply. The hoped-for result is

$$\begin{array}{cc} \uparrow & \uparrow \\ M\ V & = P\ Q \end{array}$$

In practice it is more likely to be

$$\overset{\uparrow}{M} \ V = \overset{\uparrow}{P} \ \overset{\uparrow}{Q}$$

C. Hyperinflation

In the United States the rate of inflation between 1952 and 1967 varied between 0.9 and 3.4 percent per annum. After 1967 inflation began to accelerate, reaching an annual rate of 10.0 percent in 1974, a figure that was regarded by all as much too high.[3] In other countries and other time periods, however, prices have sometimes risen by thousands, millions, and even billions of percentage points per year, a situation known as hyperinflation. The classic example is found in the Germany of the early 1920s. With massive unemployment and widespread poverty, the German government was afraid to raise taxes, and financed its expenditures, as governments are prone to do in such circumstances, by printing money. With the economy disrupted by the war, there was little scope for real output to increase, and prices began to rise.

$$\overset{\uparrow}{M} \ V = \overset{\uparrow}{P} \ Q$$

After a while prices began to rise so fast that the decline in the value of the German currency, the mark, began to affect people's behavior. They wanted to spend their marks as soon as they got them, before their value decreased. Marks passed from hand to hand at a faster and faster pace. Velocity began to increase.

$$\overset{\uparrow}{M} \ \overset{\uparrow}{V} = \overset{\uparrow}{P} \ Q$$

A double-acting engine pumped prices higher and higher, and the process began to feed on itself—the situation known as hyperinflation. At its height, German workers insisted on being paid twice daily, so that they could spend the wages due them in the morning before prices rose in the afternoon. The German middle class was wiped out as its savings and pensions became worthless. Usually hyperinflation ends in social breakdown. In the German case it, and the ensuing widespread unemployment, paved the way for Adolf Hitler.

---

3. Source: *Economic Report of the President*, 1977, p. 191.

III.   BANKS AND BANKING

Because demand deposits make up about 75 percent of the money stock, in order to understand at a more sophisticated level the workings of monetary policy, it is necessary to know something about the banking system. The number of banks in the United States is measured in the thousands, in marked contrast to most other countries where a small number of banks have hundreds of branches from one end of the country to another. Britain has three major banks; Canada less than a dozen. While the Bank of America has hundreds of branches in California, that is exceptional. In most states, one branch is all that is permitted. The courts in Florida have ruled that a bank may not have a safe-deposit box in a supermarket where customers might drop off deposits, on the ground that it was in effect a branch of the bank, and Florida law does not permit branch banking.

Laws such as these, which prevent banks from realizing economies of scale and add millions of dollars per year to the cost of doing business, date from the days when the frontier was a reality, and newly arrived settlers in the South and West feared the economic power of New England bankers. Laws forbidding branch banking were meant to curb the power of the banks, but, as is so often the case, all they really do is protect the inefficient from the competition of their more energetic rivals.

Another difference between American practice and that found elsewhere is that all of the other major financial powers have a central bank, an organ of government[4] where banks may make deposits, which is responsible for the conduct of monetary policy, and which keeps an eye on monetary relations with other countries. The Bank of England, the Bank of France, and the Bundesbank in Germany all fill this role for their respective countries. There is no "Bank of the United States" in this sense. There are, in fact, twelve separate banks, located around the country in the major financial centers: New York, San Francisco, Kansas City, Minneapolis, etc. Each is known as a Federal Reserve District Bank and plays the role of central bank for the banks in its area. Having twelve centers instead of one reflects again the American distrust of concentrated financial power.

Their activities are coordinated by a Federal Reserve Board, which has its headquarters in Washington, D.C., whose chairman has

---

4. An exception is the Bank of England, which from its founding until the end of World War II was privately owned.

sometimes been referred to as the second most powerful person in the country. The Federal Reserve Board, often called the "Fed" for short, is America's central bank.

IV. THE MECHANICS OF BANKING

Let us follow the fortunes of a mythical J. P. Smith as he opens a new bank in a fast-growing suburb of Los Angeles. Smith cannot open a bank whenever and wherever he wishes. Banking is a heavily regulated industry. He must first obtain a charter, either from the federal government, in which case his bank must be a member of the Federal Reserve System, or from a state government, in which case membership is optional. Banks with federal charters can often be identified by the word *national* in their title; First National Bank of Boston, for example. Having obtain a charter, Smith opens his doors for business on a sunny first of July.

After a while, in walks Ernest Jones, who wants to open a checking account. Smith congratulates him on being the bank's first customer, gives him a checkbook, and accepts $4000 as an initial deposit.

To keep the example simple, let us assume that Jones is the only customer on July 1. After closing the doors at the end of the business day, Smith makes the first entry in the account book as follows:[5]

J. P. Smith Bank ASSETS		July 1 LIABILITIES	
Reserves	$4000	Demand deposits	$4000
	$4000		$4000

Smith drives home whistling a cheery tune. Things have gone well on his first day in business. He has accepted his first customer, his accounts balance, and he is in compliance with the law that requires him to keep reserves in the form of cash in the vault (vault cash) or on deposit at the Federal Reserve District Bank equal to at least 20 percent of demand deposits (the actual reserve requirement is not 20 percent, but this is an easy figure to work with). In fact Smith has reserves in the form of vault cash equal to 100 percent of

---

5. Actually the account would be much more complex than this. The value of the bank building would appear as an asset; the capital Smith had subscribed would appear as a liability. These items have been omitted in the interests of simplicity because they do not affect the main argument.

the demand deposits, a very comfortable margin indeed, he tells himself.

Seated behind his desk on the morning of July 2, Smith does not see things quite so rosily. The electricity and telephone bills are due at the end of the month, and he is not earning any money. His ruminations are interrupted by the entry of Diana Robinson, who asks if she can take out a loan of $16,000 to buy a new Mercedes. Smith, who knows that Robinson, a prosperous local businessperson, is a good credit risk, does a quick calculation, and says that he will be delighted to oblige. He opens a checking account for Robinson and at the close of business amends the account as follows:

J. P. Smith Bank ASSETS		July 2 LIABILITIES	
Reserves	$4,000	Demand deposits	$20,000
Loan	$16,000		
	$20,000		20,000

That night Smith's mood verges on euphoria. His accounts balance, he has reserves of exactly 20 percent of demand deposits, and he has made his first loan to a very good credit risk; at 8 percent, the loan will bring in $1280 over the next year.

In the meantime, Robinson has made a visit to the automobile dealer, written a check for $16,000, and driven home to show off her new possession to an admiring family. The dealer deposits the check in the dealership account at the Second National Bank, which, in turn, deposits it in its account at the Federal Reserve District Bank in San Francisco.

Monday, July 5, turns out to be a very blue Monday indeed for J. P. Smith. In the mail is a letter with a San Francisco postmark containing Robinson's check. The Federal Reserve Bank requires $16,000 right away to cover it. There is $4000 in vault cash, but that is not nearly enough. There is an unpleasant feeling in the pit of Smith's stomach.

Since this is a hypothetical example, and not the cruel world of reality, we can give Smith a second chance by wiping out all the transactions that occurred after the close of business on July 1. Let us assume that, as before, Robinson walks in on July 2, but this time asks to borrow only $3200 to finance a Ford Pinto as a graduation gift for her eldest daughter. Smith gladly makes the loan, and the accounts for that day read as follows:

J. P. Smith Bank ASSETS		July 2 LIABILITIES	
Reserves	$4000	Demand Deposits	$7200
Loan	$3200		
	$7200		$7200

Now when the letter from San Francisco arrives, Smith can send off $3200 from the vault cash, leaving the account like the following:

J. P. Smith Bank ASSETS		July 5 LIABILITIES	
Reserves	$ 800	Demand deposits	$4000
Loans	$3200		
	$4000		$4000

Both reserves and Robinson's account have been reduced by $3200, and reserves are exactly 20 percent of the demand deposits.

To make the example more general, refer back to the July 1 account. With demand deposits of $4000, required reserves are equal to 20 percent of that figure, or $800. Actual reserves are $4000 and excess reserves $4000 − $800 = $3200. This is the figure that may be lent out, and it was fortuitous that this was the amount Robinson wanted to borrow.

V. BANKS AND THE MONEY SUPPLY

Now let us examine J. P. Smith's activities from a slightly different viewpoint. What has been their effect on the nation's money supply? A moment's thought will provide the answer: nothing at all. All that has happened is that Ernest Jones's $4000 in cash has been taken out of circulation and replaced by a $4000 demand deposit. But J. P. Smith's bank does not make up the entire banking universe. Let us examine the accounts of the Second National Bank, where the car dealer deposited Diana Robinson's check. Again, for the sake of simplicity, we will not show any other entires relating to other transactions.

Second National Bank ASSETS		July 2 LIABILITIES	
Reserves	$3200	Demand deposits	$3200
	$3200		$3200

Demand deposits at the Second National, and hence the money supply, have increased by $3200. But even this is not the end of the story. Second National now has excess reserves equal to the following:

$3200   − $3200 × 0.20   = $2560

(Reserves)   (Required reserves)   (Excess reserves)

and may make a loan, if the suitable opportunity arises, equal to that amount. Through a similar process to that already described, yet a third bank will have an increase in demand deposits of $2560 and excess reserves of the following:

$$\$2560\ (1 - 0.20) = \$2560 \times 0.80 = \$2048$$

Theoretically the expansion of the money supply can proceed indefinitely through fourth, fifth, and further banks, but since the increased demand deposits get smaller and smaller, they make up an infinite series with a finite sum. The total increase in the money supply resulting from Jones's $4000 deposit is the following:

$$\$4000 + \$3200 + \$2560 + \$2048 + \ldots$$

$$= \$4000\ (1 + 0.8 + 0.8^2 + 0.8^3 + \ldots)$$

If these numbers seem familiar it is because we met a similar series in Chapter 5 in our discussion of the multiplier. By using the same procedure as we did then, it can be shown that the sum of the series is equal to the following:

$$\$\frac{4000}{1 - 0.8} = \$\frac{4000}{0.2} = \$20,000$$

More generally, if the reserve requirement is R,[6] a deposit of D can increase the money supply by

$$\Delta M = \frac{D}{R}$$

While a single bank, acting on its own, cannot increase the money supply as a result of a cash deposit, it can set in motion a train of events whereby the banking system as a whole can do so. In fact, if the J. P. Smith bank had been a monopoly, i.e., that one bank had

---

6. R is a number between 0 and 1. If the reserve requirement is 20 percent, $R = 0.2$.

been the entire banking system, then it could have loaned Robinson $16,000 on July 2 as in our first example. All the checks in the chain would simply result in additions to, or subtractions from, various individual demand deposits, the overall figure of $20,000 remaining unchanged.

At least that would be the case if two implicit assumptions that have been made were valid. In our example, every check written was deposited in a bank; every bank with excess reserves loaned them out. It might well be that someone in the chain would choose to take cash instead of depositing a check, or some banker might choose to let excess reserves remain inactive instead of lending them. If there is leakage into cash or excess reserves, the multiple expansion of the money supply comes to an abrupt halt. The formula we derived should be regarded as an upper limit. The actual expansion of the money supply will almost certainly be less.

VI.   BANK FAILURES AND FINANCIAL PANICS

In the nineteenth century bank failures were a common phenomenon. Before the formation of the Federal Reserve System, a small town bank would keep its reserves, over and above the vault cash needed for its day to day operations, on deposit with one of the large New York banks. It sometimes happened that a rumor would spread that the small-town banker was in trouble, and customers began to fear the loss of their deposits. So began a process that often led to their fears being fully justified. Suppose the bank's account looked like the following:

Small-Town Bank ASSETS	($ millions)	February 1, 1878 LIABILITIES	
Reserves	4	Demand deposits	14
Loans	10		
	—		—
	14		14
	—		—

Panicky depositors clamored to withdraw their deposits, standing in a line that stretched from the teller's window, through the front door of the bank, halfway down the block. Early arrivals got their money from vault cash. Those farther down the line received cash derived from checks drawn on the New York Bank. Some of the banker's loans were fairly liquid—that is, readily convertible into cash (U.S. treasury bills for example)—and the sale of such securities took care of the withdrawals of more bank customers.

After all of the transactions described above were completed, the account read something like the following:

Small-Town Bank ASSETS		February 5, 1878 LIABILITIES	
Reserves	0	Demand deposits	8
Loans	8		
	—		—
	8		8
	—		—

With depositors still clamoring for their money, with the remaining loans outstanding uncollectible, or not due to be repaid until some time in the future, the small-town banker might try to borrow funds in order to keep afloat. Should the banker find this impossible—and at this stage the bank is not a particularly good credit risk—the banker would have no recourse but to close the doors and declare bankruptcy.

A. Financial Panics

If the scenario outlined above happened to a large number of banks, a financial panic would occur. With small-town banks from all over the country withdrawing reserves, the large New York correspondent banks would also be in trouble. Bank failures would be widespread, and as each door closed, thousands, or millions, of dollars in demand deposits would be extinguished, and the money supply would decline precipitously. A calamity in the financial sector would become a calamity for the whole business sector as output and prices fell.

$$\downarrow \quad \downarrow \downarrow$$
$$M \ V = P \ Q$$

B. The Lender of Last Resort

In such circumstances, Walter Bagehot, a nineteenth-century British writer on economics, advocated that one of the duties of a central bank should be to become a "lender of last resort." If banks could obtain reserves nowhere else, the central bank should make them available. Even after the formation of the Federal Reserve in 1913, however, bank failures still occurred, and reached epidemic proportions in the early 1930s, at the beginning of the Great Depression.

C. The Federal Deposit Insurance Corporation

Something further was needed. In 1933 the Federal Deposit Insurance Corporation (FDIC) was established as an arm of the federal government to insure bank customers against the loss of their deposits in the event of their bank failing. Today those deposits are insured up to a maximum of $100,000. The mere existence of the FDIC means that it is not often called on to reimburse depositors for losses because, knowing that their deposits are safe, depositors do not rush to withdraw funds at the first sign of trouble. Since World War II, only a few banks have failed, and usually they have opened again under the management of trustees appointed by the FDIC, or a merger has been arranged with a stronger bank. Depositors have suffered a minimum of inconvenience and have not lost a penny. The only exception has been the unlucky depositors of small state-chartered banks that were not members of the FDIC.

VII. SUMMARY AND CONCLUSION

Money serves as a medium of exchange, a store of value, a unit of account, and a standard of deferred payment. Broadly defined, anything that is accepted as money is money. More narrowly, in the United States of today, the most commonly accepted definition (M_1) is the sum of currency and demand deposits.

The quantity equation of exchange is a simple tool that gives us some valuable insights into the role of monetary policy in combating inflation and unemployment, as well as an explanation for inflation itself.

The banking system is of great interest to the macroeconomist because of its role in the creation of money. During and prior to the 1930s financial panics occurred when depositors withdrew large amounts of funds from the banking system, but because of the existence of the Federal Reserve Board and the FDIC the probability of a financial panic occurring today is minimal.

QUESTIONS

1. Use the quantity equation of exchange to illustrate suitable monetary policies to combat:
    (a) Unemployment.
    (b) Inflation.
         In each case name one probable undesired side effect.
2. A bank has reserves of $380,000 and demand deposits of $1,000,000. The

reserve requirement is 17 percent. What is the maximum sum the bank can lend out?
3. Define the terms:
   (a) M₁.
   (b) M₂.
   (c) Velocity of circulation.
   (d) Excess reserves.
   (e) Leakage into cash.

8 | The Rate of Interest

We have spent some time discussing the first and last of the three economic variables in *The General Theory of Employment, Interest and Money.* In this chapter and the next we will discuss the middle variable and its relationship to the other two.

In Keynesian analysis the rate of interest is determined by the interaction of the supply of and the demand for money.

I. THE MONEY SUPPLY

The money supply is determined by the Federal Reserve, which from time to time announces its targets for the rate of growth of M_1 and M_2. In 1979 these were, respectively, M_1, 1.5–4.5 percent per year; and M_2: 5–8 percent per year. The Federal Reserve has been unable to control the money supply with any great degree of precision. Indeed, more often than not, it receives a great deal of criticism for failing to maintain its targeted growth rates. Nevertheless, the mechanisms it uses in the control process are extremely important.

To illustrate the three major tools of monetary policy, we need to look at two accounts: the consolidated balance sheets of banks that are members of the Federal Reserve Systems and that of the Federal Reserve itself. The accounts below are hypothetical. Many items have been left out and the figures, in billions of dollars, have been chosen for ease of exposition.

All Member Banks ASSETS		May 1, 1979 LIABILITIES	
Reserves	60	Demand deposits	300
Loans	240		
	300		300

Federal Reserve ASSETS		May 1, 1979 LIABILITIES	
Government securities	60	Member bank reserves	60
	60		60

Assuming a reserve requirement of 20 percent, it will be seen that the banking system has no excess reserves. The major liabilities of the Federal Reserve are the reserves of its member banks, which, it will be recalled, are held largely in the form of deposits at the Federal Reserve District Banks. The Federal Reserve's major asset is a portfolio of government securities.

A. Open-Market Operations

To increase the money supply, the Federal Reserve, acting through the instrumentality of its New York district bank, located in the heart of the nation's financial district, buys government bonds from one or more bond dealers, and pays for them by writing checks which the bond dealers deposit in their bank accounts. In turn, these checks are credited to the banks' accounts at the New York district bank. Again, for ease of exposition, we show the Federal Reserve buying bonds worth \$2 billion—a much larger quantity than would normally be the case. Reflecting these transactions, the accounts now read as follows:

All Member Banks ASSETS		May 2, 1979 LIABILITIES	
Reserves	62	Demand deposits	302
Loans	240		
	302		302

Federal Reserve ASSETS		May 2, 1979 LIABILITIES	
Government securities	62	Member bank reserves	62
	62		62

Demand deposits, and hence the money supply, have increased by $2 billion. With a reserve requirement of 20 percent, the banks may now make further loans until demand deposits total

$$ \$ \frac{62}{0.2} = \$310 \text{ billion} $$

Assuming that the banking system makes all the loans to which it is legally entitled, the member banks' account becomes

All Members Banks ASSETS		May 31, 1979 LIABILITIES	
Reserves	62	Demand deposits	310
Loans	248		
	310		310

The money supply has increased by a further $8 billion, or $10 billion in all.

To decrease the money supply, the Federal Reserve District Bank in New York sells bonds, decreasing bank reserves and forcing a multiple reduction in the money supply.[1] If it sold bonds worth $2 billion, the final accounts would be:

All Member Banks ASSETS		June 30, 1979 LIABILITIES	
Reserves	58	Demand deposits	290
Loans	232		
	290		290

---

1. To assist in understanding this process, the reader may work out the intermediate steps as an exercise.

Federal Reserve ASSETS		June 30, 1979 LIABILITIES	
Government securities	58	Member bank reserves	58
	58		58

To help the reader remember the relationship between the purchase (or sale) of bonds and the increase (or decrease) in the money supply, the following will be found useful:

Bonds out (of private ownership)   Money in (circulation)
Bonds in   Money out

This monetary policy tool is known as "open market operations." Because the Federal Reserve can buy or sell ten, a hundred, or thousands of bonds, it may be used to make quite small adjustments to the money supply. It is therefore the most important and widely used tool in the Federal Reserve's monetary policy kit.

It might seem at first that increasing and decreasing the money supply are perfectly symmetrical operations, the only difference being the substitution of the phrase *buy bonds* for *sell bonds* or vice versa. This is not so. When the sale of bonds by the Federal Reserve causes a contraction in member bank reserves, the banks, once their excess reserves are used up, have no option but to call in some of their loans, thus reducing demand deposits and the money supply. A Federal Reserve purchase, on the other hand, makes excess reserves available, but the banks now have a choice: to make more loans, thus expanding the money supply, or simply to let the excess reserves sit there, in which case no multiple expansion in the money supply occurs.

Would rational profit-maximizing banks act in this way? They might. An expansionary monetary policy is presumably undertaken to fight recession, precisely the time when there are not too many eager borrowers around, and those that are tend to be less than desirable credit risks. Someone once aptly summed up the difference in the phrase "You can't push on a string." The Federal Reserve is much more able to induce a contraction in the money supply than to engineer an expansion.

B. A Change in Reserve Requirements

The second tool of monetary policy is seldom used. When it is, the Federal Reserve really means business, since it can only be used to cause quite large changes in the money supply. A change in the reserve requirement is the sledgehammer; openmarket operations the diamond cutter's mallet.

Refer back to the first account where the reserve requirement was 20 percent. The Federal Reserve is free to change that requirement within certain broad limits set by Congress. Usually the changes are of the order of ½ or 1 percent, but, again, for ease of exposition, we will work through the effects of a change of 5 percent.

Suppose that the reserve requirement were increased to 25 percent. The Federal Reserve account is immaterial, we will just show the member banks' account.

All Member Banks ASSETS		May 15, 1979 LIABILITIES	
Reserves	60	Demand deposits	240
Loans	180		
	240		240

The increased reserve requirement forces the member banks to reduce their demand deposits to $240 billion, which they do by reducing their loans to $180 billion. A good banker will have loans due for repayment at varying points in time. Loans maturing when the reserve requirement is increased may therefore simply not be renewed, or the banker may sell a portion of the portfolio of government bonds. The effect of an increase in the reserve requirement is to decrease the money supply.

If the reserve requirement is reduced to 15 percent, banks are free to expand their loans until their demand deposits reach $400 billion. The account then reads as follows:

All Member Banks ASSETS		May 28, 1979 LIABILITIES	
Reserves	60	Demand deposits	400
Loans	340		
	400		400

A quick calculation shows that 60 is exactly 15 percent of 400.

Again, an increase in reserve requirements represents pulling on the string; a decrease is a push. With the first, banks must reduce their loans; with the second, they may increase them, but the choice is theirs.

C. A Change in the Discount Rate

From time to time a bank will find itself with insufficient reserves relative to its volume of demand deposits. At the same time, there may be no loans falling due for repayment and it may be inconvenient, or the bank may not want, to reduce its portfolio of government bonds. What can it do? There are two alternatives.

It may borrow funds from another bank that has excess reserves, perhaps for two or three days, or even overnight. It does this in a market called the federal funds market, and pays a rate of interest called the federal funds rate.

Its second option is to borrow reserves from the Federal Reserve itself. Again, it pays interest on its borrowings, this time at a rate called the discount rate. A low discount rate tends to encourage bank borrowings; a high rate discourages them. Actually, the Federal Reserve is in a stronger position than simply being able to raise or lower the discount rate. It can say, "Yes, you may borrow needed reserves," or "No, you may not." For this reason the discount rate is the least important of the three monetary policy tools. The Federal Reserve tends to use it passively, keeping it in general alignment with other rates of interest, usually a fraction of a percentage point below the federal funds rate. It may also employ it as a signal to the financial community, an increase in the discount rate signaling a restrictive monetary policy in the weeks ahead; a decrease is a sign that an expansionary policy is contemplated.

II.   THE DEMAND FOR MONEY

Why do people want money? It may seem an obvious question, but the answer is actually quite complex. The simple-minded response is that to have large quantities of money is to be wealthy, which gives the wealth-holder command over goods and resources, and perhaps political and other forms of power.

But wealth need not be held as money. Bonds, stocks, land, real estate, stamps, old masters, rare books—the list is almost infinite. And money is sterile—the holder receives no return on it. Indeed there is a cost involved in holding money, an opportunity cost. Wealth-holders who purchase stocks or bonds receive dividends, interest, and/or capital gains that are foregone when money is held. Why then do people hold money? There are three basic reasons, which give rise to three sources of demand for money.

A. Transactions Demand

Families and individuals receive their income at regular intervals, usually weekly or monthly. Their expenditures, by contrast, are made throughout the week or month. They need to hold money to take care of their expenditures from one payday to the next. Money held in this fashion is used for transactions and gives rise to a transactions demand.

The amount of money needed for this purpose will vary with the frequency of receipt of income and with income. Since frequency of payment changes only over long intervals of time, transactions demand (L_t) is a function of income.

$$L_t = f(Y)$$

B. Precautionary Demand

Imagine going on a summer vacation to the coast. Halfway to your destination your car breaks down, and the repair bill takes all the spare cash you have with you. Your vacation ruined, you return home.

Had you had some extra cash with you to take care of the unexpected eventuality, you might have proceeded on your way, with the vacation spoiled only by the delay on the journey.

The money you carry as a precaution against the unforeseen gives rise to a precautionary demand. Its need has diminished with the growing use of widely accepted credit cards, and for analytical purposes it will be consolidated with the third category of demand.

C. Speculative Demand

You think that the stock of the Ford Motor Company will perform well over the next two years. It is currently selling for $50 per share and you have $5000 available which you plan to put into the stock market. What do you do?

You might buy 100 shares of the stock right away for $5000. If over the next month the stock falls to $40 per share, you would have to buy it, but have no money available to do so. Now suppose that you had not bought the stock when it was selling at $50, but kept your money in your checking account. When the stock falls to $40 you can purchase 125 shares and congratulate yourself on being a smart operator. Of course, if the stock has risen to $62.50, you could only buy 80 shares and would be kicking yourself for not having bought at $50.

When you hold money in the hope of purchasing some asset at a lower price than that at which it is currently selling, you are speculating that its price will fall. Hence the term *speculative demand for money.*

The quantity of money held for both precautionary and speculative purposes depends on the cost of holding it, the opportunity cost represented by the interest that might have been earned had the money been invested in an earning asset. Using the symbol L_s for the speculative demand—with which we lump the precautionary demand—for money,

$$L_s = F (i)$$

where i = interest rate.

D. The Demand for Money: The Keynesian Approach

In *The General Theory* Keynes developed a simple model in which wealth might be held in only two forms: money and bonds. To understand his approach, therefore, it is necessary to know something about the bond market.

E. Bonds

When you buy a bond you are lending money to the corporation or government agency that issues the bond. The issuer promises to pay interest on the bond at an agreed on rate and to repay the principal, usually $1000, after an agreed period of time. For example, a corporate bond paying $60 per year when first issued in 1978, to be repaid in 2008, and selling for $1000, has a maturity of thirty years and pays 6 percent. The only commitment the issuer of the bond makes is to pay $60 per year for thirty years, and to repay the principal thirty years from the date of issue. If the corporation fails in either of these commitments, the bank that acts as the representative of the bondholders may take it to court and have it declared bankrupt.

The rate of interest paid upon the bond—6 percent in the above example—depends on three major factors:

1. The length of time to maturity. The longer this period is, the higher the rate of return the lender expects.[2]
2. The risk associated with the bond. A bond issued by the United States government, with its tremendous reserve of taxing power, is virtually riskless. The securities of large corporations—AT&T, Du Pont, and Exxon—do not have quite the same factor of safety, but are of very high quality. Smaller less profitable corporations, have a much higher probability of eventually going bankrupt. Their bonds are less safe, and so the interest that they pay must include a risk premium.
3. The rate of inflation. When prices are rising rapidly, lenders know that

---

2. It sometimes happens that, when interest rates are very high, the short-term rate may be greater than the long-term rate. This is an exceptional state of affairs. Normally the long-term rate exceeds the short-term rate.

the dollars that they receive when their bonds mature will be worth considerably less than the dollars they lent. To protect themselves against the loss of purchasing power they demand higher interest rates than when prices are stable. Borrowers also recognize that they will pay off the bondholders with less valuable dollars, and so will be willing to pay the higher interest rate.

In the United States it appears that over long periods of time investors expect a real rate of return on their bonds of about 3 percent per year. The rates of interest paid by three categories of thirty-year bonds might be broken down as follows:

RATE, %	REAL RATE OF RETURN, %		RISK PREMIUM, %		INFLATION PREMIUM, %		NOMINAL INTEREST RATE, %
U.S. Treasury	3	+	0	+	5	=	8
AT&T	3	+	1	+	5	=	9
Philadelphia Electric	3	+	3	+	5	=	11

In what follows we assume that the various bonds mentioned all carry the same degree of risk.

Suppose that in 1978 the ABC corporation issues a thirty-year bond with a promise to pay $60 per year until maturity. The rate of interest is 6 percent, and the relevant facts are summarized in the first line of Table 8−1.

In 1979 interest rates rise, perhaps because the rate of inflation is on the increase. The JKL corporation, which issues another thirty-year bond in that year, finds it has to offer an interest rate of 7 percent; it must pay $70 per year on a $1000 bond.

Now suppose that the buyer of the ABC bond, perhaps because of an unexpected illness in the family, is forced to sell the bond in 1979. The corporation is under an obligation to pay off the bond before 2008, but active markets exist in New York where bonds may be bought and sold upon payment of relatively small commissions. Can the bondholder expect to receive the $1000 paid in 1978?

The answer is clearly no. With the JKL bond of similar quality paying $70 per year, no one will pay $1000 for a bond only returning $60 per year. The bond may be sold, but only by accepting something less than the original purchase price, perhaps $950. The important point is that when interest rates rise, bond prices fall.

Table 8-1   Relationship Between Bond Prices and Interest Rates

CORPORATION	YEAR OF ISSUE	PRICE OF BOND	ANNUAL INTEREST PAYMENT	YIELD, %	YEAR BOND MATURES
ABC	1978	$1000	$60	6	2008
JKL	1979	$1000	$70	7	2009
XYZ	1980	$1000	$50	5	2010

Another year passes and interest rates fall. The XYZ corporation goes to market in 1980 and finds it need pay only $50 per year on a $1000 bond. The owner of a JKL bond who was forced to sell in 1980 would be in for a pleasant surprise. With a comparable bond paying only $50, the annual return of $70 looks very attractive. The owner will find buyers willing to offer more than $1000 for the bond, perhaps as much as $1100. When interest rates fall, bond prices rise.

F. The Demand for Money Again

Returning now from our digression on bonds, consider a wealth-holder who has to make the decision on whether to hold it in the form of money or bonds. Suppose that interest rates are low, 3 percent, say. Isn't a return of 3 percent, as low as it may be, preferable to the return of zero obtained by holding money? Keynes's answer as no. With interest rates low, there is not much room for them to go lower, and the probabilities are that they will rise. Rising interest rates, as we have just seen, mean falling bond prices. The bondholder forced to sell will incur a capital loss that may well be greater than the amount of interest so far received. It is better to hold money than bonds; the speculative demand for money is high.

Conversely, when interest rates are high, the high rate of return makes bonds attractive. Furthermore, with rates high, there is more room for them to go lower, and if they do the bondholder will see the value of the security rise. Bonds are doubly attractive, both because of their high yield and because of the prospect of a capital gain. The other side of the coin is that at high rates of interest the speculative demand for money is low.

Figure 8−1a shows the relationship between speculative demand and the interest rate that follows from the above analysis. As the rate of interest declines, the quantity of money demanded for speculative purposes increases, and at a sufficiently low rate the risk of a capital loss becomes so great that wealth-holders will buy no more bonds. At that rate of interest the speculative demand function

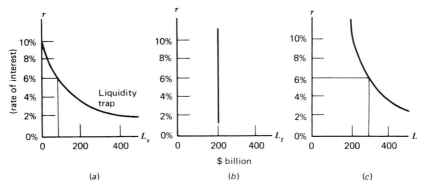

Figure 8-1. *(a)* **Speculative demand** *(Lₛ).* *(b)* **Transactions demand** *(Lₜ).*
(c) **Total demand** $(L = L_t + L_s)$.

becomes horizontal. Keynes called that portion of the function the
"liquidity trap."[3] It will play a very important role in later analysis.

The transactions demand, which is dependent on the level of
income, is assumed independent of the interest rate. The transactions demand function will therefore be as depicted in Figure 8−1b.
It is drawn assuming that income stays constant. Should income
increase, the function will shift to the right; if it declines, the
function moves leftward.

The total demand for money

$$L = L_t + L_s$$

is derived in Fig. 8−1c. At interest rates above 10 percent speculative demand is zero; total demand coincides with transactions
demand. At an interest rate of 6 percent, total demand is equal to the
sum of L_t = $200 billion and L_s = $80 billion. At 2 percent the
speculative demand function becomes horizontal; so does the total
demand function.

What determines the interest rate in the Keynesian system?
Supply and demand. Not the supply of and demand for loanable
funds as in Chapter 2, but the supply of and the demand for money.
Figure 8-2 illustrates the question.

If the Federal Reserve sets the money supply at $250 billion,
supply and demand are in equilibrium at an interest rate of 4

---

3. Fewer economists today believe in the existence of a liquidity trap. Because of its importance
   in the development of the Keynesian argument, however, a student of macroeconomics must
   be familiar with the concept.

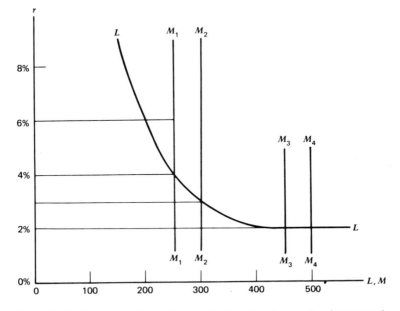

Figure 8-2. Determination of interest rates in a Keynesian framework.

percent. If the interest rate happens to be 6 percent, supply exceeds demand. Wealth-holders exchange money for bonds; they buy bonds. Buying increases the demand for bonds, raising their price. Remembering that bond prices and interest rates move in opposite directions, interest rates fall to the equilibrium level. At an interest rate of 3 percent, the demand for money exceeds the supply, and wealth-holders sell bonds to obtain the needed money balances. Selling increases supply, depressing bond prices, and interest rates rise to the equilibrium level.

If the Federal Reserve increases the money supply to $300 billion, the supply of money exceeds the demand and the interest rate falls to 3 percent. In addition, the Federal Reserve increases the money supply by buying bonds, raising their price, and this contributes to the fall in interest rates.

When interest rates reach 2 percent, it does not matter how much the money supply is increased—from M_3 to M_4, for example—the interest rate can decline no further. In the liquidity trap, wealth-holders simply hold the newly created money. The fear of incurring a capital loss prevents them from buying bonds and lowering the interest rate any further.

III.   SUMMARY AND CONCLUSION

The Federal Reserve has three major tools for the conduct of monetary policy: (1) open-market operations; (2) a change in reserve requirements; and (3) a change in the discount rate. The first is used on a day-to-day basis, the second is seldom used but has a great impact when it is, and the third is now used largely as a signaling device to the financial community.

The demand for money may be broken down into three components: (1) a transactions demand; (2) a precautionary demand; and (3) a speculative demand. For analytical purposes the second and third of these can be consolidated.

In the Keynesian system the interest rate is determined by the interaction of the supply of and the demand for money. The first of these is determined by the Federal Reserve and the second by decisions by wealth-holders as to the relative attractiveness of money vis à vis bonds.

QUESTIONS

1.

All Members Banks ASSETS		June 1, 1980 LIABILITIES	
Reserves	528	Demand deposits	3300
Loans	2772		
	3300		3300

Federal Reserve ASSETS		June 1, 1980 LIABILITIES	
Government securities	528	Member bank reserves	528
	528		528

Above are the relevant portions of the acounts for all member banks and the Federal Reserve. The reserve requirement is 16 percent. Suggest suitable policies for decreasing the money supply by $100 billion;
(a)   Through the use of open-market operations.
(b)   Through a change in the reserve requirement.

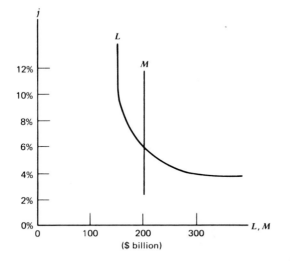

Figure 8-3.

2. In Fig. 8–3,
   (a) What is the equilibrium level of i?
   (b) If $i = 8$ percent, what will wealth-holders do in a Keynesian framework?
   (c) What will be the effect of their actions?

9 | A Synthesis

In Chapters 5 and 6 we examined the market for goods and services, observed how the interaction of aggregate supply and aggregate demand determined the equilibrium level of income, and studied the various facets of fiscal policy. Chapters 7 and 8 introduced money, showed how supply and demand in the money market affected interest rates, and described how the Federal Reserve conducts monetary policy. The question now arises as to whether these topics are separate, as we have so far implicitly assumed, or whether disturbances in the goods market have repercussions in the money market, and/or vice versa.

In the pre-Keynesian era the answer would have been a qualified no. Then it was believed that the market for goods and services, the "real" economy, was independent of the money market. Money was seen as a veil that while it made the observation of the real economy more difficult, did not affect it in any material way.

If the price of milk is $1 per gallon, and cabbages are $0.50 per pound, then one gallon of milk exchanges for two pounds of cabbages. That is the important consideration. If the money supply is now doubled, the price of milk rises to $2 per gallon, and cabbages sell for $1 a pound, but the exchange ratio of one gallon of milk for two pounds of cabbage is unaffected. When M doubles, P doubles, and the price of all individual goods and services doubles, leaving the real relationships between them unchanged. The quantity equation of exchange tells all.

$$\overset{\uparrow}{M} V = \overset{\uparrow}{P} Q$$

Keynes believed that money was more than a veil, and that what happens in the money market does affect the goods market in a significant fashion. Specifically he argued for a relationship between one variable in the goods market—investment—and another in the money market—the rate of interest. Let us now examine that argument in detail.

I.   INVESTMENT AND THE RATE OF INTEREST

The management of a firm is considering its expenditures on investment for the coming year. Three projects look feasible. One, representing an investment of $100,000, has an estimated return of 8 percent. A second, with a price of $200,000, looks as if it will return 6 percent, while the third costs $150,000 and returns 4 percent. The three possibilities are illustrated diagrammatically in Fig. 9–1. Which projects should be undertaken? Which shelved?

The answer depends on the rate of interest. If it is 9 percent, none

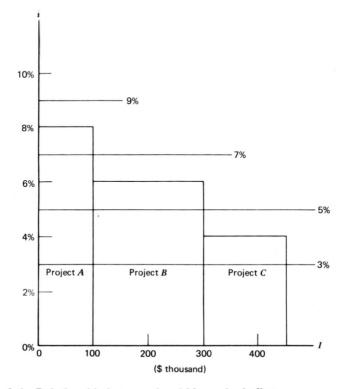

Figure 9-1.   Relationship between *I* and *i* for a single firm.

of them will receive a stamp of approval. Why borrow at 9 percent when the expected return is less than that? Note that even if the firm can generate all the necessary funds internally, without recourse to banks or the bond market, the answer is the same. It pays to put those excess funds into the bond market at 9 percent rather than to accept a lesser return. There is an opportunity cost involved, even for firms that are flush with cash.

If the interest rate is 7 percent, Project A becomes viable. It is worthwhile to borrow at that rate to fund a project that returns one percentage point more. Projects B and C, however, are still not worthwhile. At 5 percent the firm will go ahead with both A and B, but not C, while at 3 percent all three projects are viable. Table 9–1 summarizes these considerations.

As the rate of interest falls, investment spending increases. What is true for one firm is true for all, and aggregate investment increases as the interest rate declines. The only difference is that instead of measuring investment in hundreds of thousands of dollars, as in Fig. 9–1, it is measured in billions. Figure 9–2 is drawn as a continuous function, rather than the step function of Fig. 9–1, because the addition of a single project on the smaller scale of that diagram makes only an infinitesimal difference to the level of aggregate investment. The diagram shows a linear relationship for the sake of simplicity. It need not be. All that matters is that it slope downward from left to right.

The main outlines of the Keynesian model are now in place. The manner in which monetary policy operates may be depicted simply.

To increase the level of economic activity, increase the money supply, or, more realistically, increase its rate of growth.

$$M\uparrow \rightarrow i\downarrow \rightarrow I\uparrow \rightarrow Y\uparrow \qquad \text{Multiplier}$$

To slow the rate of economic activity, decrease the money supply, or, as was remarked in Chapter 7, since this would be rather drastic medicine, decrease its rate of growth.

$$M\downarrow \rightarrow i\uparrow \rightarrow I\downarrow \rightarrow Y\downarrow \qquad \text{Multiplier}$$

Table 9-1   Relationship Between Investment and the Interest Rate

RATE OF INTEREST, %	TOTAL INVESTMENT
9	$0
7	$100,000
5	$300,000
3	$450,000

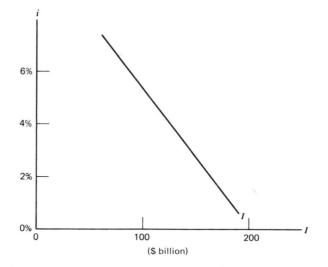

Figure 9-2. Relationship between aggregate investment and the interest rate.

II.   A MORE COMPLEX INTERACTION

While we have established a link between the rate of interest and the level of investment—between the money market and the goods market—the interaction is actually more complex than that. Suppose the Federal Reserve increases the money supply. Interest rates fall and investment increases. Through the multiplier effect GNP increases, and with it the transactions demand for money. With the demand for money increasing, interest rates rise again. Some of the initial impact is offset. These more complex interactions can be handled by an apparatus developed, not by Keynes, but by one of his successors at the University of Cambridge, Sir John Hicks. Once again, to introduce the analysis at a simple level, we assume that there is no government sector. That can be added later.

III.   THE *IS* CURVE

In the simple analysis of Chapters 5 and 6, saving was assumed to be a function of income, while investment, independent of income, was constant. Now we know that investment depends on the rate of interest; to assume investment is constant is to assume that the rate of interest is constant. Our goal now is to analyze what happens in the goods market when both income and the interest rate are free to vary. Once again the price level is assumed constant.

In Fig. 9–3, quadrant *A* shows the saving function of Chapter 4. Since it would take a very deep depression indeed to reduce aggregate saving to a negative level, it only shows the part of the function that lies above the *Y*-axis. We may chose any starting point on the *Y*-axis. Let us pick $600 billion. Saving, read from the vertical axis, is $50 billion.

Quadrant *B*, with saving on the vertical axis and investment on the horizontal axis, plots all values of *S* and *I* for which the equilibrium condition *S* = *I* holds. All such points, of course, lie on a 45 degree line from the origin, as we have seen before. The thin line transfers the $50 billion figure from quadrant *A* to quadrant *B*. Investment must also be $50 billion in equilibrium, and this is shown on the horizontal axis.

Quadrant *C* follows the pattern of Fig. 9–2, showing investment as an inverse function of the interest rate. Investment of $50 billion

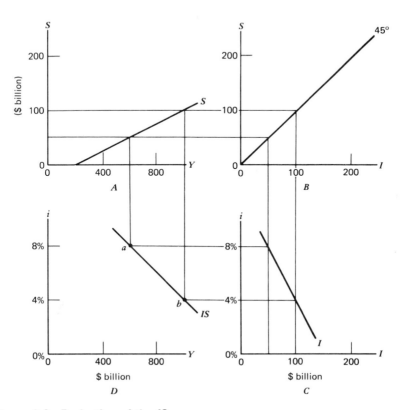

Figure 9-3. Derivation of the *IS* curve.

will be undertaken if the interset rate is 8 percent, and this may be read off the vertical axis.

Quadrant D has income on the horizontal axis and the rate of interest on the vertical. By transferring the value of Y down from quadrant A and the rate of interest across from quadrant C, we obtain one point—point a—where the levels of Y and i are consistent with equilibrium; that is, they result in equal amounts of saving and investment.

Starting with another value of Y in quadrant A—$1000 billion— and tracing around the four quadrants as before, we obtain another combination of Y and i consistent with equilibrium—point b. Since all our functions are linear, and two points are sufficient to determine a straight line, we may simply draw a straight line through points a and b in quadrant D. That line is called the IS curve, meaning that it passes through all the combinations of Y and i that result in the equality of S and I.

Instead of having a single equilibrium level of Y, as in Chapter 5, we now have a combination of various values of Y and i that result in equilibrium in the goods market. At point a, for example, where Y, and hence S, is relatively low, i needs to be high, so that I is also low. At point b, on the other hand, Y and S are high, so i needs to be low to make I high. With an infinite number of equilibrium combinations, which is the one toward which Y and i will gravitate? To answer that question, we must transfer our attention to the money market.

IV.   THE LM CURVE

Again the analysis involves a four-quadrant diagram (Fig. 9–4). Quadrant A shows the transactions demand for money as a linear function of income. The line starts from the origin because when Y = 0, L_t is also equal to zero. Following a similar procedure to that for deriving the IS curve, we note that when Y = $400 billion, L_t = $80 billion.

Quadrant B shows the relationship between L_t and L_s for a given money supply, in this instance $200 billion. If all of the $200 billion is held in the form of transactions balances, L_s = 0. This gives us the intercept on the vertical axis. Conversely, if all of the available money supply is held in the form of speculative balances, L_t = 0. The intercept on the horizontal axis is also $200 billion. Other possible combinations of L_t and L_s lie on a straight line joining these two intercepts, a line making a 45 degree angle with both axes.

Transferring the value of L_t from quadrant A to quadrant B, we

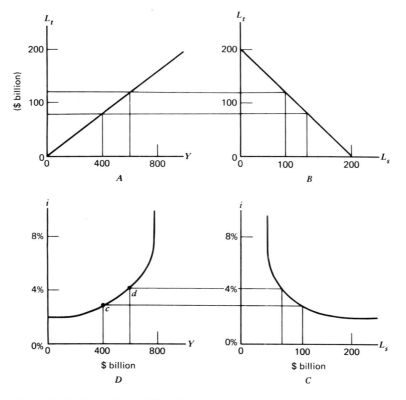

Figure 9-4. Derivation of the LM curve.

may read off the corresponding value of L_s ($120 billion), and note that $L_t + L_s = \$(80 + 120 = 200)$ billion. The demand for money is equal to the supply, the money market equilibrium condition.

Quadrant C shows the speculative demand function, with its liquidity trap, that we discussed in Chapter 8. A value of L_s of $120 billion is consistent with an interest rate of 2.8 percent.

Projecting the value of Y downward from quadrant A, and the vaue of i across from C, the intersection of the two thin lines gives us one combination of Y and i at which the money market is in equilibrium—point c. By following a similar procedure, starting at other values of Y in quadrant A, we obtain a series of points in quadrant D that represent money market equilibrium. Point d, for example, is dervied by starting at $Y = \$600$ billion. The line through these points is known as the LM curve, since it defines all the combinations of Y and i at which the demand for money (L) is equal to the supply (M).

There are an infinite number of such points, and the question again arises, to which of them is the money market attracted? The answer is simple. We plot the IS and LM curves on the same diagram (Fig. 9–5). The goods market is in equilibrium anywhere on the IS curve; the money market anywhere on the LM curve. Both markets are in equilibrium where the two curves intersect, and this is the equilibrium point toward which the economy tends to move.

V.   POLICY IMPLICATIONS

The analysis may now be used to investigate the effects of monetary policy. If the money supply is increased to $230 billion, the function in quadrant B (Fig. 9–6) shifts outward, so that both intercepts are $230 billion. By tracing around the four quadrants as before, but using this function instead of the original one, a new LM curve may be derived that intersects the IS curve at E_2. Y increases as in our earlier analysis, from $620 to $640 billion, but not by as much as it would have had the interest rate remained constant. In that case it would have expanded to $660 billion. Why is this! A portion of the increase in the money supply is held in the form of idle speculative

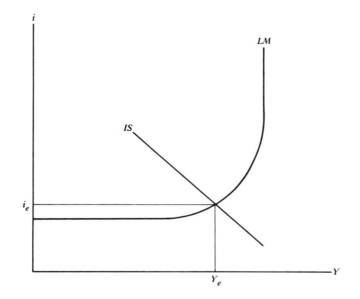

Figure 9-5. Determining the equilibrium values of Y and i.

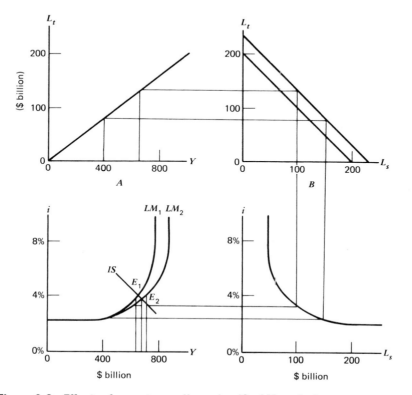

Figure 9-6. Effects of monetary policy using *IS−LM* analysis.

balances. Put another way, with part of the money stock not cir-
culating, velocity declines. Some of the increase in M is offset.

$$\underset{M}{\uparrow} \; \underset{V}{\downarrow} \; = \; \underset{Y}{\uparrow}$$

The reader is urged to trace the effects of a decrease in the money
supply to make the analysis more easily understood.

To analyze the impact of fiscal policy with the $IS-LM$ model we
need to recall the result derived at the end of Chapter 6.

$$S + (T - G) = I$$

which redefined the equilibrium condition of saving and planned
investment so that saving was made up of two components: private
saving (S) and government saving $(T - G)$.

No change need be made in Fig. 9−3, except to redefine saving to
include government saving. An increase in government spending,

through decreasing $T - G$, shifts the saving function downward by an amount equal to ΔG. This shifts the IS curve to the right (Fig. 9–7), increasing GNP and raising the rate of interest.

The increase in Y is not as great as it would have been had the interest rate remained constant. The additional government borrowing required to finance the increased deficit, with G increasing and T constant, squeezes out some investment. Note that it is implicitly assumed that the deficit is not financed through an increase in the money supply; otherwise the LM curve would also shift.

The full government-spending multiplier effect may be achieved if fiscal policy is coordinated with monetary policy. If the money supply is expanded just sufficiently to hold the interest rate constant, then Y expands by the full amount $\Delta G/(1 - c)$.

The reader may work out the effect of a tax cut on the IS curve. Remember that a tax cut decreases government saving by ΔT, shifting the saving function downward by that amount, but increases

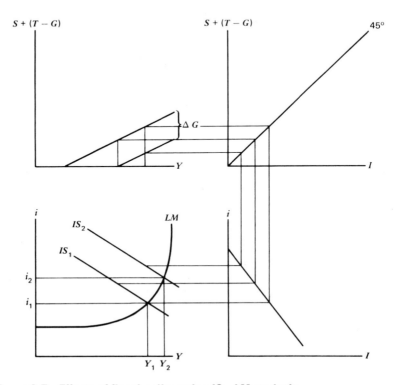

Figure 9-7. Effects of fiscal policy using *IS—LM* analysis.

private saving by $s\Delta T$. The net effect is to lower the saving function by

$$\Delta T - s\Delta T = (1 - s)\,\Delta T = c\Delta T$$

which is consistent with our earlier result that the tax multiplier is smaller than the government-spending multiplier.

VI.   THE EFFICACY OF FISCAL AND MONETARY POLICY

The *LM* curve has three major segments (Fig. 9–8). Keynes believed that the horizontal portion, reflecting the existence of the liquidity trap, was the relevant range in the depths of a deep depression, hence it is often called the Keynesian Range. Fiscal policy, whether through an increase in government spending or a cut in taxes, results in the *IS* curve moving to the right, from IS_1 to IS_2. The full multiplier effect is obtained; there is no increase in interest rates to choke off investment.

In the vertical segment, fiscal policy is completely ineffective. An expansionary policy, shown by the shift in the *IS* curve from IS_5 to IS_6, simply raises interest rates. Y does not increase at all. This segment, it will be recalled, reflects the situation where interest

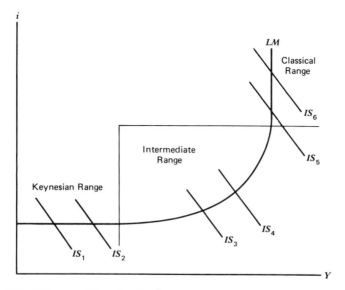

Figure 9-8. Efficacy of fiscal policy.

rates have become so high that the speculative demand for money is nonexistent. Since the extreme Classicists do not believe in the existence of a speculative demand for money, this range is called the Classical Range. In it, an increase in government spending, or an increase in consumption resulting from a tax cut, is completely offset by a decline in investment.

In the segment joining the horizontal and vertical segments, the Intermediate Range, fiscal policy is partially effective, but not so effective as in the Keynesian Range. Some of the effect of an increase in G is offset by a decline in I, but not all. The multiplier effect is reduced, but not eliminated.

What has just been said about fiscal policy is true also of monetary policy, but in reverse. If the IS curve intersects the LM curve in the Keynesian Range (IS_1 and LM_1 in Fig. 9–9), an increase in the money supply, which moves the LM curve to LM_2, will have no effect whatever on Y. All of the additional money created remains idle in speculative balances.

In the Classical Range (IS_3 and LM_1), monetary policy has its maximum effectiveness. The entire increase in the money supply, which causes the LM curve to move from LM_1 to LM_2, goes into transactions balance. There is no speculative demand at these high interest rates. Conversely, if the goal is to reduce aggregate demand

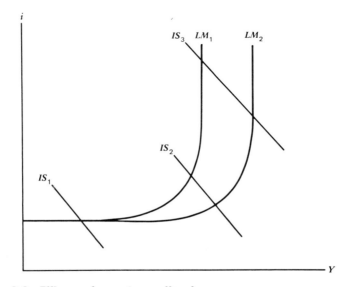

Figure 9-9. Efficacy of monetary policy: I.

in the face of inflationary pressures,[1] monetary policy is the preferred instrument. The move from LM_2 to LM_1 has the maximum
effect on Y.

In the Intermediate Range (IS_2 and LM_1), monetary policy has
some effect, but since some of the newly created money, which
causes the LM curve to shift rightward, is absorbed in speculative
balances, the effect is not so great as it is in the Classical Range.

Shifting our attention to the IS curve, the closer it is to the horizontal (IS_1 in Fig. 9–10), the more effective monetary policy will be:
the closer to the vertical, the more ineffective (IS_2). Some, but not
all, Keynesians regard IS_2 as the more likely case, hence the
emphasis they put on fiscal policy in all phases of the business cycle.
Those who believe that IS_1 is more typical advocate the use of fiscal
policy to fight recession; monetary policy to moderate inflation.
This last view corresponds most closely with the inclinations of
politicians. Tax cuts and government spending increases to fight
recession are politically popular; tax increases and spending cuts to

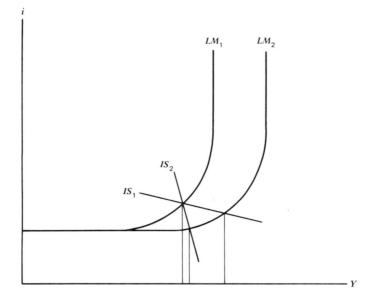

Figure 9-10. Efficacy of monetary policy: II.

---

1. There is an obvious contradiction in discovering inflation in a model in which the price level is
   assumed constant. Given a choice between rigor and simplicity, the latter must take priority
   in an elementary text.

battle inflation are not. Small wonder that they prefer to let the
Federal Reserve take the heat for the unpopular moves that are
necessary to bring inflation under control.

VII.   THE RIGHT MIX OF FISCAL AND MONETARY POLICY

Economic planners considering a suitable mix of fiscal and monetary measures to bring aggregate demand to a level consistent with
full employment and stable prices actually have an infinite number
of choices, two of which are depicted in Fig. 9–11. Which fiscal
monetary mix is preferred, that reflected in the intersection of IS_1
and LM_1 or that typified by IS_2 and $LM_{|2}$? To achieve full employ-
ment of resources, either will do. But there may be other pressing
economic problems than full employment and stable prices. The
choice can then be made on the basis of these other concerns.

IS_1 and LM_1 represent a combination of a relatively restrictive
fiscal policy and an expansionary monetary policy. The former, particularly if it is a result of higher taxes on the household sector,

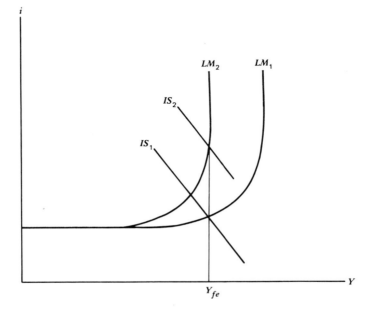

Figure 9-11. Determining the right mix of fiscal and monetary policy.

restricts consumption; the latter stimulates investment. The combination is an appropriate strategy for economic growth.

IS_2 and LM_2 represent the reverse: an expansionary fiscal policy offset by tight money. As Fig. 9–11 shows, this policy mix results in higher interest rates than the other, higher interest rates that can attract funds from abroad to strengthen a weak currency. The value of the dollar today is determined, as is the value of most things, by supply and demand. High interest rates in the United States induce foreign as well as American investors to buy U.S. bonds. In order to buy U.S. bonds, foreigners need dollars, the purchase of which increases demand, driving up the price of the dollar vis à vis other currencies.

This chapter, and the three that preceded it, analyzed policies on the implicit assumption that the major problem to be dealt with is either unemployment or inflation, a perfectly reasonable assumption for the thirty years preceding 1966. Since then, however, we have seen both unemployment and inflation at unacceptably high levels at the same moment in time. What does the economist have to say about this dual problem, and what, if anything, can be done about it? That is the subject of the next chapter.

VIII.   SUMMARY AND CONCLUSION

In a Keynesian framework, monetary policy affects the level of economic activity through its effect on the rate of interest, the level of investment, and the multiplier.

$IS-LM$ analysis provides a vehicle for analyzing the complex interaction between the goods market and the money market. It enables us to evaluate the efficacy of fiscal and monetary policies at different levels of Y and i, as well as how to use those policies to achieve other objectives than full employment and stable prices.

Economic growth may be stimulated through encouraging investment at the expense of consumption, while high interest rates can attract funds from abroad to strengthen the dollar.

QUESTIONS

1. The management of a firm is considering three possible capital expenditures: (1) the purchase of a machine at a cost of $200,000 with an expected rate of return of 8.5 percent. (2) The purchase of a heavy-duty ore transporter at a cost of $350,000 with an expected return of 7.75 percent; (3) upgrading existing machinery at a cost of $215,000 with an

expected return of 9.25 percent. What will the firm's investment expenditures be if the rate of interest is:

(a)   10 percent.
(b)   9 percent.
(c)   8 percent.
(d)   7 percent.

2. Draw four quadrants on a sheet of graph paper as per Fig. 9—3; make four copies.

   (a)   On copy 1 derive the *LM* curve. Add an *IS* curve to the fourth quadrant. Show the effect on Y and i of a decrease in the money supply.

   (c)   On copies 2, 3, and 4, derive the *IS* curve. Add an *LM* curve to the fourth quadrant. Show: the effect of a tax increase; the effect of a tax cut; and the effect of a decrease in government spending.

10 | Inflation and Unemployment

Earlier analysis made a simplifying assumption: there is one level of GNP (Y_{fe}) at which all resources are fully employed. Whenever GNP is at a lower level, the problem to be tackled is unemployment; whenever it is higher, our efforts must be directed toward fighting inflation. The goal of economic policymakers is to get GNP equal to Y_{fe}. That, the theory developed so far tells us, is Nirvana—a happy state in which there is neither unemployment nor inflation. The theory is elegant and simple; the theory is also unsatisfactory. It has one glaring defect: it is inconsistent with the world of reality.

A step in the right direction leads to the replacement of a single-valued Y_{fe} with a full-employment zone (Fig. 10-1). When aggregate demand is increased by suitable policy measures from $(C + I + G)_1$ to $(C + I + G)_2$, the resulting increase in Y consists entirely of an increase in real output. Our earlier assumption that the price level remains constant is valid. As aggregate demand increases still further, however, to $(C + I + G)_3$, the increase in real output is accompanied by a rising price level. The deeper into the full-employment zone one gets, the greater the proportion of the increase in Y because of a rising price level, and the smaller the real output component. In moving from $(C + I + G)_3$ to $(C + I + G)_4$, for example, while some increase in real output is obtained, most of the increase in Y is because of an increase in prices. Once the right-hand edge of the zone is reached, no further increase in output is possible. All of the increase in Y when aggregate demand moves from $(C + I + G)_4$ to $(C + I + G)_5$ is because of inflation.

This theoretical construct has been borne out by empirical

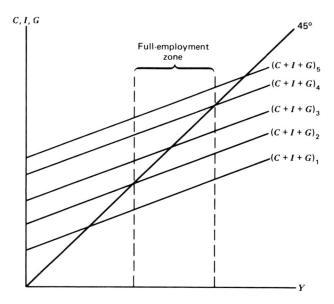

Figure 10-1. Full-employment zone.

research. A.W. Phillips, an Australian economist, studied the relationship between inflation and unemployment in the United Kingdom for almost a century,[1] and found that, at least for the period of his study, the relationship remained fairly stable (Fig. 10-2). Since Phillips's original study, other researchers have found similar patterns for other countries, including the United States.

Phillips's findings have been rationalized as follows: when unemployment is high, workers are concerned with retaining their jobs. They do not rock the boat by pressing for large wage increases. At the same time, employers, faced with weak markets, have difficulty selling the goods they produce and do not have too much to lose from a strike, should one be forced on them. In such circumstances the rate of increase in wages, and hence of costs, tends to be low, prices rise slowly and, if the rate of unemployment is sufficiently high—above 8 percent in Fig. 10-2—may even decline. By contrast, when the rate of unemployment is low and the economy is hum-

---

1. A.W. Phillips, "The Relation between Unemployment and the Rate of Change in Money Wage Rates in the United Kingdom, 1862–1957," *Economica*, November 1958, pp. 283–299. As its title indicates, Phillips's study was concerned with the rate of change of wage rates, rather than with inflation. Since these variables are closely correlated, however, the substitution of the latter for the former has become a common practice.

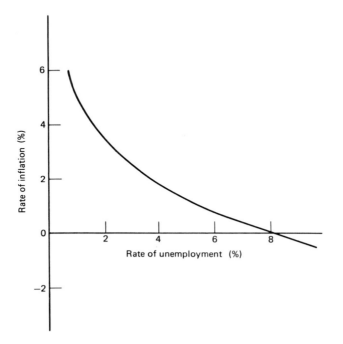

Figure 10-2. Phillips curve.

ming along nicely, workers have no compunction in asking for substantial wage increases. Employers, not wishing to lose the advantage of their strong markets and loath to take a strike, grant most of their employees' demands, knowing that the resulting higher costs can be passed along in the form of higher prices.

Once the existence of the Phillips curve had become accepted, the role of the macroeconomist was to prescribe suitable fiscal and/or monetary policies, designed to bring the economy to whatever point on the curve the people, acting through their elected representatives, decided was optimal. It was recognized that the Nirvana of zero inflation and zero involuntary unemployment was unattainable, but that unemployment could be reduced, if so desired, at the cost of experiencing a slightly higher rate of inflation. If inflation was thought to be too high, that could also be taken care of at the expense of a small rise in the number of the unemployed. In the early 1960s the belief was almost universal among economists that the economy could be fine-tuned in this manner.

In the 1970s that belief was shattered. The Phillips curve began to drift outward (Fig. 10-3), so that whereas in 1967 it was possible to

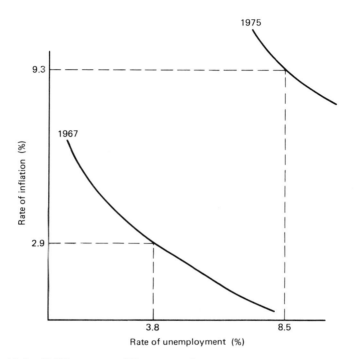

Figure 10-3. Phillips curve shifts outward.

have an unemployment rate as low as 3.8 percent along with an inflation rate of only 2.9 percent, by 1975 unemployment at the uncomfortably high level of 8.5 percent was accompanied by a torrid rate of inflation 9.5 per cent.[2] "Back to the drawing boards" became the catchphrase among economists as the soul-searching of the 1970s replaced the euphoria of the 1960s.

The major difference between the experience of earlier periods and that of the 1970s is that in the former inflation came in short bursts, whereas in the latter it has been a sustained phenomenon. The sharp inflation of 1942, for example, was followed two years later by a rise in the price level of only 2 percent. Double-digit inflation in 1946 and 1947, a result of the release of the purchasing power pent up during World War II, was followed by a 1 percent decline in the price level in 1949. Since 1968, by contrast, the inflation rate has never fallen below 4 percent.

---

2. Source: *Economic Report of the President*, 1977, pp. 191 and 221.

Sustained inflation gives rise to the expectation of further inflation, and expectations influence behavior patterns. Some economists argue that there is a "natural rate" of unemployment, influenced not only by the level of frictional unemployment, but also by the composition of the labor force, particularly by the proportion of married women and teenagers. Controversy surrounds the exact percentage level of the natural rate, but almost all agree that it is higher today than it was in the early 1960s. Rates of 5.5 percent today and 4 percent for the earlier period are perhaps not too far from the mark. This natural rate of unemployment, the rate to which the economy tends to return, is shown in Fig. 10-4 at the former figure.

The manner in which the natural-rate concept—sometimes referred to as the "long-run Phillips curve"—can generate either stable or outward-moving Phillips curves proceeds somewhat as follows. Suppose that the rate of inflation is 2 perent, and unemployment is at the natural rate of 5.5 percent (point 1 in Fig. 10-4). In an attempt to reduce the level of unemployment, government undertakes stimulative fiscal and/or monetary policies to bring it down to 4

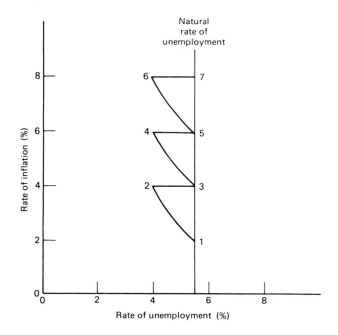

Figure 10-4. Natural rate of unemployment.

percent. The goal is achieved at the cost of driving the inflation rate up to 4 percent (point 2).

Government concern now shifts to the inflation rate. Policies designed to bring it back to 2 percent succeed, but only by increasing unemployment to the original level of 5.5 percent (point 1 again). The movements from point 1 to point 2, back to 1, again to 2, and back to 1, appear to be movements along a stable Phillips curve.

But what if government, having brought the economy to point 2, attempts to keep it there? Inflation continues at the 4 percent rate until workers, seeing their real wages declining, insist on restoring them to their original levels. Faced with a higher wage bill, employers lay off workers and the economy moves to point 3.

Still considering a 5.5 percent unemployment rate too high, government again implements stimulatory policies, which succeed in moving the economy to point 4. Now the forces brought into being at point 2 against become operative and the economy moves to points 5, 6, and eventually 7. The unemployment rate is where it was originally at point 1, but the rate of inflation is at 8 percent instead of 2. The Phillips curve appears to have moved outward, away from the origin, from point 1 to point 7.

What policy measures are appropriate for the world of simultaneous inflation and unemployment? Economists have a variety of answers. The following represent only a sampling of some of the major viewpoints.

I. ELIMINATE INFLATIONARY EXPECTATIONS

Because continuing inflation influences human behavior in an undesirable manner, the important policy goal is to eliminate that inflation, even at the cost of a fairly severe recession. Proponents of this policy argue that the social costs resulting from the economic downturn represent the price that must be paid for the earlier mistake of permitting inflation to get out of hand. Once the rate of change of the price level has been brought down to the average of 2 percent or so that prevailed in the 1950s, and has remained at that level for some time, the actors on the economic stage will adjust their roles to the new circumstance. Workers will not demand huge wage increases as an insurance against an anticipated loss of purchasing power; corporations will not raise their prices to recover expected increased costs. The economy will have returned to its more normal condition of low unemployment and low rates of inflation, a state of affairs well worth the price that must be paid.

II.   UNEMPLOYMENT AS THE MAJOR PROBLEM

While unemployment and inflation are the major economic problems of our time, some economists take the view that inflation is, at worst, something of a nuisance, whereas unemployment makes the lives of those affected completely unbearable. The policy prescription resulting from this line of thought is to use stimulative fiscal and monetary policies whenever the unemployment rate rises above some predetermined level, regardless of what the rate of inflation may be. Perhaps a majority of economists would argue that such a policy must be self-defeating, since the higher and higher rates of inflation that necessarily follow inevitably culminate in a recession of much greater proportions than might have occurred in the absence of economic stimulation.

Consumers, seeing a continuously rising price level, step up their purchases, believing that what appears to be expensive today will be even more expensive in the future, and plunge deeper into debt to do so. Business owners, seeing the value of their inventories rise, and perhaps having difficulty in getting supplies as the economy approaches the full-employment level, begin stockpiling inventories. Both forms of behavior represent borrowing from the future. At some point, having decided that they have acquired all the durable goods and inventory that they need, both groups cut back their expenditures. The decision to cut back is made easier by rising interest rates, propelled upward by growing inflation premiums, which increase the cost of debt to the consumer and of carrying inventories to businesses. Aggregate demand declines and a recession is underway, a recession that lasts longer than it otherwise would because households and businesses are well stocked with durables and are busily repaying debt—in other words, increasing saving and reducing consumption and investment.

III.   WAGE AND PRICE CONTROLS

The type of inflation discussed in earlier chapters is often called demand-pull inflation, because it results from excess aggregate demand. In the language of Chapter 6, there is an inflationary gap at the full-employment level of GNP. The price level is pulled upward by excess demand, hence the term *demand-pull.*

Another type of inflation may be recognized, "cost-push" inflation, so called because the causal factor is increasing production costs, associated with a rising wage bill, as powerful trade unions push wages ever higher.

For obvious reasons, some labor leaders put the blame for cost-push inflation on greedy corporations seeking to increase profits in imperfectly competitive industries. This approach confuses "high" prices with "rising" prices. While it is true that prices tend to be higher in imperfectly competitive industries than they would be if perfect competition prevailed, once prices have reached the profit-maximizing level,[3] any higher price would so adversely affect the quantity demanded that total profits would fall. If its costs rise, of course, a firm does have an incentive to reduce its output and raise its price, but then it is simply reacting to pressures originating in the labor market. It transmits the forces of inflation; it does not cause them.

Figure 10-5 shows that if labor unions force an increase in the wage rate from $6 to $7 per hour, unemployment increases from 600 to 1200.[4] To be sure, unemployed workers may seek employment in the nonunionized sector, but labor is not perfectly mobile. Many of the unemployed remain in their own localities, waiting for their employers to recall them, and the existence of unemployment compensation reduces the urgency of finding new employment.

In 1979 the labor unions in the rubber and automobile industries negotiated huge wage increases at a time when the demand for tires and automobiles was declining, making unemployment in those industries greater than it would have been as a result of declining demand alone.

The higher wage bill causes firms to raise their prices. Since cost-push inflation causes both unemployment and inflation, it explains the real world of the 1970s better than its demand-pull counterpart.

Other sources of the cost-push inflation experienced in the 1970s include the more than 1000 percent increase in oil prices pushed through by the OPEC cartel, higher food prices as foreign buying has pushed up the price of wheat and feed grains, and a cyclical upswing in cattle prices that has raised the price of beef.

Cost-push inflation cannot persist for any length of time without the covert cooperation of the Federal Reserve. If, seeing unemployment on the rise, the Fed permits the money supply to grow at a faster rate to "validate" the wage and price increases, unemploy-

---

3. Students who have taken microeconomics will recognize this as the point where marginal cost equals marginal revenue.

4. Full employment is determined by the intersection of supply and demand at a wage rate of $5 per hour. At $6 per hour employers want to hire 2000 workers, while 2800 are seeking work. At $7 per hour, 3100 workers are competing for the 1900 jobs that employers are offering.

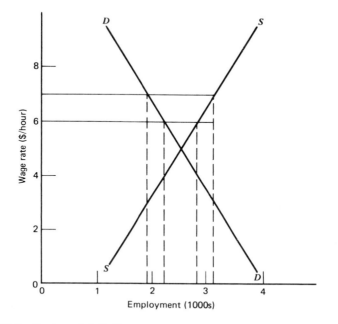

Figure 10-5. Cost-push inflation.

ment will be temporarily reduced, setting the stage for yet another round of increases. No matter what form inflation may take, it can be ended whenever the growth of the money supply is brought under control. Former chairman of the Federal Reserve William McChesney Martin aptly described the Fed's role in controlling inflation as "taking away the punchbowl when the party is just beginning to warm up." But a tight-money policy will only end inflation at the cost of a rise in the unemployment rate, at least in the short run. Hence the rationale for wage and price controls.

Proponents argue that wage increases need not be inflationary so long as they are offset by increased productivity, defined in terms of output per worker. If, for example, wages are increased by 4 percent at the same time that each worker produces 4 percent more output on the average, then labor costs per unit of output do not increase, and prices need not rise.

When, on the other hand, wages increase faster than productivity, then costs per unit of output increase, which puts pressure on the price level. The solution to the problem of cost-push inflation, therefore, is to limit the rate of increase in wage rates to the rate of increase in productivity plus the rate of inflation toward which policymakers are aiming. The goal of 5 percent inflation, for example, when productivity is improving by 2 percent per year, is attainable according to this reasoning if wage increases are limited to (5 + 2 = 7) percent per year.

Since labor is a potent political force, the wage restraint would probably be accompanied by restrictions on allowable price increases to give the appearance of even-handed treatment as between business and labor. In this example, price increases would be limited to 5 percent per year.

The restraint on wages and prices may be voluntary, in which case reference is made to *wage-price guidelines*, or compulsory, when the term *wage-price controls* is used. Nixon used compulsory restraints; Carter preferred a voluntary system, but made use of all the power of the federal government, its procurement policies, publicity, and so on, to see that people adhered to the guidelines.[5]

Wage-price controls have a superficial appeal. Indeed, in 1979 a majority of Americans believed that such controls were the best policy to combat inflation. But controls suffer from the same defect as all remedies that seek to treat the symptoms of a disease, rather than the disease itself. The imposition of wage-price controls by government is analogous to the actions of a doctor, who, required to cure a patient with a temperature of 103°F, pays more attention to the thermometer than to the patient. Rising prices are only a symptom of an underlying malaise. Just as the doctor needs to examine the patient and not the thermometer, so too the economist must see beyond the rising price level to the underlying forces that are propelling it higher.

This is only the beginning of the case against controls. In seeking to stabilize a macroeconomic variable, the average price level, one necessarily puts restraints on the prices of individual goods and services, and those prices fulfill an important microeconomic function, serving as a very efficient signaling mechanism. Higher prices say produce more, consume less. Lower prices do the reverse. By means of those signals, resources are allocated efficiently. Let us examine this question in more detail.

If the controlled price is above the free-market equilibrium price (Fig. 10-6a), controls have no effect. The ceiling of $4 is above the free-market price of $3 that prevails. But when controls have been in effect for some time in an inflationary environment, the rise in money income causes the demand curve to shift upward, while the

---

5. This was written in early 1980. Some observers expected that this so-called voluntary system was only a step on the way to mandatory controls.

supply curve is raised too by increasing costs. Eventually the situation depicted in Fig. 10-6*b* becomes typical, and shortages develop. Consider the effect of all this on someone with a small home-building business.

Such a person is very good at building houses, but in an era of shortages, the person spends less time doing the thing using that skill and more time attempting to cope with the shortage of supplies. The builder telephones distant lumberyards when the local supplier runs out. Even when supplies are located in distant markets, however, the expense of trucking them to the building site raises costs.

The situation is made worse if, as is likely to be the case, exports are exempted from price controls in an attempt to improve the balance of payments deficit, or to strengthen the weak dollar that invariably accompanies domestic inflation. Given a choice of selling abroad for whatever the market will bear, or selling at home for the lower controlled price, profit-maximizing entrepreneurs ship their products overseas, worsening the domestic shortage. This was a common occurrence during the era of the Nixon controls.

In a word, controls lead to inefficiency, when, to combat inflation, what is needed is an increase in efficiency and a reduction in costs.

It might be argued that the above criticisms are strictly applicable to a regime of permanent wage and price controls. The longer they are in effect, the greater the distortions that they cause. While this argument does have an element of truth in it, temporary controls have their disadvantages, too. Goods tend to be held back from the market in the hope of selling them at higher prices when the con-

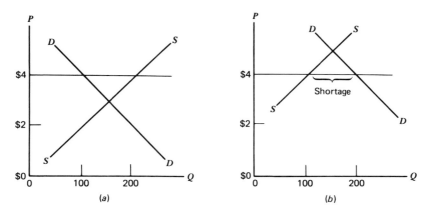

Figure 10-6. Price controls engender shortages.

trols are lifted, intensifying the controls-induced shortages. (Some observers believe that the gas lines of June 1979 were lengthened by oil companies holding back gasoline in anticipation of the partial decontrol of oil prices set for July 1 of that year.) When the controls are eventually lifted, the resulting jump in prices takes them to a higher level than they would have reached had the controls not been imposed in the first place, a necessary result of the inefficiencies caused by restrictions on the free functioning of the market system.

Finally, wage-price controls have an additional drawback that makes the case against them overwhelming: merely discussing them produces the disease that proponents argue that they can cure. Fearing the imposition of controls, firms raise their prices in order to do today what may be illegal, or frowned upon, tomorrow. Workers seek large wage boosts for the same reason.

Economists know that wage-price controls are bad news. One of their major tasks is to convince politicians and the people who vote for them that this is indeed the case.

IV.   INDEXING

Since one side effect of programs designed to stimulate the economy and reduce unemployment is an increase in the rate of inflation, some observers have concluded that inflation has become a fact of life. They argue further that while inflation cannot be eliminated, it can be made less intolerable through indexing incomes to the price level. If, for example, policymakers decide that real wages should rise by 2 percent on an annual basis, and the rate of inflation is 8 percent, they simply decree that money wages go up by (8 + 2 = 10) percent. Planning for bondholders to receive a real rate of return of 3 percent, the issuers of bonds are required to pay interest equal to (8 + 3 = 11) percent for that particular year.

Again, the proposal has a superficial appeal, but also a fatal flaw. Once inflation develops, indexing, through increasing costs, virtually ensures that the inflation will continue indefinitely. Furthermore, not all income recipients can be protected. Profits are a residual. Higher wages and interest costs mean lower profits, a state of affairs that bodes ill for investment. Or consider a small private college whose faculty's salaries are indexed to the rate of inflation. While the tuition rate can be increased by an appropriate amount, there is no way that students can be forced to attend the college if they do not wish to, no way of ensuring that the income from the endowment fund keeps pace with inflation, and certainly no way of inducing college alumni to increase their giving in proportion to the increased costs.

V. REPEAL OF LEGISLATION THAT IS INFLATIONARY AND/OR MAY INCREASE UNEMPLOYMENT

In their search for solutions to the problem of combined inflation and unemployment, economists have been taking a new look at the results of existing legislation, some of which has been on the statute books since the 1920s. Among the major causes for concern are the following.

A. The Minimum Wage

Legislation dating from the 1930s, which requires employers to pay their employees a wage no less than a prescribed minimum, is both inflationary and a major cause of unemployment among the unskilled. Particularly hard hit by it are blacks and teenagers. The law is inflationary since it raises the costs of employers of unskilled labor—operators of fast-food franchises, for example—and a cause of unemployment, since it prevents an employer who would be willing to hire a worker at a lower wage than the legal minimum from doing so.

B. The Social Security Tax

Another piece of legislation that dates from the days of the New Deal, the Social Security system, is designed to provide a source of income to workers upon their retirement. Social Security is financed by a payroll tax, half of which is paid by the employer, half by the employee. As the tax increases over time to finance benefits indexed to the rate of inflation, it increases costs, and is thus itself inflationary. In addition, it gives employers an incentive to economize on the number of workers they hire—the fewer there are on the payroll, the less tax they have to pay—and so contributes to unemployment.

C. The Davis-Bacon Act

The Davis-Bacon Act (1931) requires the secretary of labor to set wages for workers engaged in federally funded construction projects. Construction firms bidding for federal projects are required to agree in advance to pay the wage rates prevailing in their area, as determined by the secretary of labor. While the law is seemingly innocuous, indeed unnecessary, since employers would presumably have to pay the prevailing wage rates in order to attract or keep their workers, in practice things have been quite different. The wage rates chosen have almost invariably been those prevailing in the unionized sector. Often the standard laid down for a rural area is that for a large city a hundred miles distant.

One would expect the federal government to want to minimize the cost of projects paid for by taxpayers, but here is a case where the low bidder is discriminated against. Under President Nixon, the secretary of labor had been the president of a New York construction union, and may have been involved in a conflict of interest on each of the hundreds of occasions that he was required to interpret the Davis-Bacon Act.

D. The Jones Act

The Jones Act (1923) requires that goods shipped between ports in the United States be carried in American flagships—ships that are more expensive to operate than those of other nations. The Jones Act raises the price of goods that must be shipped by sea and has a particularly adverse effect on the cost of living in Alaska, Hawaii, and Puerto Rico.

E. Farm Price Supports and Crop Restriction Programs

Programs designed to raise farm incomes by means of artificially supporting the price of crops above the free-market level contribute to higher food prices, a particularly visible component of the consumer price index, since food must be purchased at frequent intervals.

F. Tariffs, Quotas, and Other Import Restrictions

Tariffs, or taxes on imported goods, raise prices directly, and quotas, which limit the quantity of a good that may be imported, through restricting supply, raise prices indirectly. Through restricting foreign competition, such measures also make domestic markets less competitive.

G. Government Regulation

Rules and regulations designed to limit entry to some industries, to prohibit advertising, and to require that certain actions be undertaken in one particular way, even though cheaper alternatives exist, restrict competition and increase costs, fueling inflation.

While economists almost universally urge the elimination of legislation that intensifies inflation and unemployment, their advice seems to fall on deaf ears. Some very powerful interests benefit from the kind of legislation just described, and politicians pay more heed to those interests than they do to much less influential economists.

VI. INFLATION AND UNEMPLOYMENT: THE FUTURE

There are signs, as this was written in early 1980, that things are changing, albeit slowly. Deregulation of the airlines is an accomplished fact. Deregulation of the railroad and trucking industries are under discussion. People in business are rebelling against the plethora of government regulations, and their elected representatives seem to be listening. It is possible to be optimistic on many of these issues as the 1980s begin.

VII. SUMMARY AND CONCLUSION

At a simple level, Keynesian analysis assumes that inflation and unemployment are alternative problems. In recent years, however, both problems have often appeared at the same point in time.

The Phillips curve shows that low rates of unemployment are often associated with high rates of inflation and vice versa. Since the 1960s, the Phillips curve, which had until then been relatively stable, began to shift outward away from the origin. This outward shift may be best explained in terms of the natural rate of unemployment and expectations of continued inflation.

Many proposals have been advanced to deal with the twin problems of inflation and unemployment: (1) eliminate inflationary expectations; (2) treat unemployment as the more serious problem and ignore the inflationary consequences of stimulatory policies; (3) control wages and prices; (4) use indexing; and (5) repeal legislation that contributes to inflation and/or unemployment.

QUESTIONS

1. (a) Outline four possible causes of cost-push inflation.
   (b) Name one economic sector that, while sometimes blamed for cost-push inflation, really only transmits it.
2. Outline five examples of government legislation that is inflationary and/or may cause unemployment.
3. Define the following terms:
   (a) Natural rate of unemployment.
   (b) Phillips curve.
   (c) Inflationary expectations.

11 | Economic Growth and the Business Cycle

In this chapter we return to two questions raised at the beginning of Chapter 5. Why does real GNP grow over time? Why does it fluctuate around the trend line? Many economists have attempted to answer one or both of these questions—too many, in fact, to enable us to give more than a brief mention to some of them. As with many economic questions, it all begins with Adam Smith (1723–1790). His discussion of specialization and the division of labor represents one of the earliest portrayals of the importance of economies of scale as a spur to growth; his attack on the heavy hand of government regulation as a brake on growth is just as relevant today as it was in eighteenth-century Britain.

I. MALTHUS THE PESSIMIST

Toward the end of the eighteenth century, a father and son, both Church of England clergymen, were in the habit of engaging in friendly argument over the breakfast table. The father, an optimist, opined that we live in the best of all possible worlds in which things can only get better. The son, Thomas Robert Malthus (1766–1834) was a pessimist, and believed that for the vast majority of English people life was hard and would remain so. So convinced was he of the truth of his beliefs that he set them down in a book, published in 1798, entitled *Essay on the Principle of Population*.

Malthus believed that people were doomed to spend their lives at the subsistence level—to have sufficient food, clothing, and a rudimentary form of shelter to them alive, but seldom much more—and that any improvements in that condition were bound to be of short duration.

Suppose that the average real wage is at the subsistence level, and that, for some reason, perhaps a succession of good harvests, the standard of living begins to rise. More and more people get married and have children. Malthus believed that what he called the "passion between the sexes" was very strong, and that the only thing that kept the working poor from having large families was the fact that they could not afford them. Their reaction to low incomes was to delay marriage. As soon as their incomes began to rise the age at which they married dropped. The interrelationships between the relevant variables are shown in Figure 11-1.

In an agricultural country, with a fixed amount of land, the law of diminishing returns prevents output from increasing in step with the growth in population. Malthus, basing his conclusions on an observation of population trends in the United States (where, at that time, land was in virtually unlimited supply), said that population tended to grow geometrically—1, 2, 4, 8, and so on—whereas output

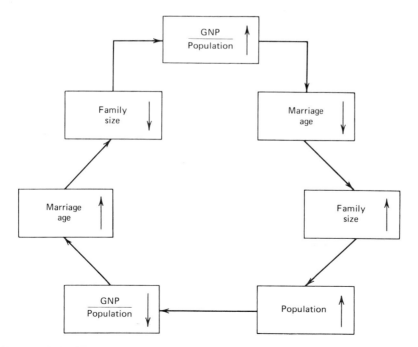

Figure 11-1. Malthusian cycle.

grew arithmetically—1, 2, 3, 4, etc.—an unnecessary refinement for his theory. All he need have said was that population tends to grow faster than output, eventually reducing GNP per capita to a level below that needed for subsistence. Now the grim reaper appears on the scene in the terrible guise of famine, war, or pestilence. As the death rate rises, population, the denominator in GNP per capita, declines, the standard of living improves, and the whole process is repeated all over again. People are doomed to spend their existence at, or close to, the subsistence level, a prediction so pessimistic in nature that Thomas Carlyle coined the phrase *the dismal science* as a description of economics.

Looking back from the vantage point of almost two centuries, we can see that Malthus's prediction was not fulfilled. The standard of living of the British worker rose almost continuously throughout the nineteenth century and into the twentieth. Clearly Malthus failed to take into account some important economic variables. We have the advantage of hindsight, but the right clues were available to Malthus and he should have seen them. When he wrote his essay, the factory chimneys were already belching smoke in the dales of Yorkshire and Lancashire. True, the land area of the British Isles was limited, but the newly settled continents of North and South America, Australia, and New Zealand had land in abundance, and their people were eager to trade their agricultural products for Britain's manufactured goods.

While Malthus may have been wrong, he was not without influence. What policy prescriptions follow from his theory that nothing can be done to improve a people's lot? Many believed that government assistance to the poor would merely exacerbate the situation, enabling them to marry earlier and have larger families. In the 1840s the British government in London did nothing while thousands of Irish died of starvation in the hedgerows and ditches of their native land when blight struck the potatoes that formed the basis of their nutritional needs. Thousands more emigrated to the United States.

Some observers believe that, while Malthus may have been wrong about his own country in his own time, his predictions may come true in the future in the world's less-developed countries if population growth is not controlled. The Sahara Desert is extending southward as overgrazing of the lands kills off the scrub and bush that held the soil in place. Famines have occurred in India and Pakistan. Yet just as new technology provided the answer in nineteenth-century Britain, it may hold the Malthusian specter at bay once again. New high-yielding crops, suitable for tropical climates, may increase the numerator of GNP per capita, while programs to disseminate information on birth control can serve to reduce the denominator. But that his theories are still discussed and believed in almost two hundred years after the publication of his essay is strong tribute to the power of Malthus's thought.

II. SAMUELSON AND THE INTERACTION OF THE MULTIPLIER AND THE ACCELERATOR

Let us assume a simple two-sector economy producing consumer goods (C) and investment goods (I). The output of consumer goods is limited only by the size of the capital stock (K), while the output of investment goods is subject to no restraint whatever. The ratio of the stock of capital to the output of consumer goods—the capital-output ratio—is constant. In symbols,

$$\frac{K}{C} = H, \text{ the capital-output ratio}$$

With all resources, including the stock of capital, fully employed, an increased demand for consumer goods will require an increase in the capital stock of

$$\Delta K = H\Delta C$$

ΔK, the change in the stock of capital in a period of one year, is simply net investment (I).

$$I = H\Delta C$$

This relationship between an increase in the level of consumption and the level of net investment is known as the accelerator principle.

A. The Interaction of the Accelerator and the Multiplier

In Chapter 5 we observed how an increase in investment could lead to a multiple increase in consumption—the multiplier. Now we have seen how an increase in consumption can lead to an increase in investment—the accelerator. Combine the two effects and it appears that we have developed a perpetual-motion machine.

Casual observation of the real world suggests that this is not the case. We see neither C nor I heading rapidly in the direction of plus infinity. This topic was investigated by Paul Samuelson (1915–), an American economist and winner of the Nobel prize. The technique he used, which involved the solution of a difference equation, would be out of place in an elementary text. We can, however, summarize his findings. As may be imagined, the outcome depends on the value of c, the marginal propensity to consume, and H, the capital-output ratio.

B. Cycles and Growth

The five possible outcomes are depicted in Figure 11-2a. *The positive quadrant of the C/H plane is divided into five segments by* three curves: $c = 1$; $c = 4H/(1 + H)^2$ (line segments B and F); and $c = 1/H$ (line segment D).

If the values of c and H are such that when plotted on Fig. 11-2a they appear in region A or on line segment B,[1] then the result is as depicted in Fig. 11-2b. An initial equilibrium situation (Y constant at a level $(Y_e)_1$, disturbed by a slight increase in some component of aggregate demand, results in a move to a new equilibrium $(Y)_2$, along a decelerating growth path. This outcome is not too surprising. It resembles a pure multiplier effect, and in this region the capital-output ratio, and hence the accelerator effect, is small.

In region C a disturbance of the initial equilibrium results in fluctuations that gradually die away (Fig. 11-2c). On line segment D (Fig. 11-2d), a disturbance of the initial equilibrium results in fluctuations of uniform amplitude, while in region E (Fig. 11-2e) we have initially small fluctuations that get larger and larger in amplitude.

In region G a disturbance results in explosive growth at an accelerating rate (Fig. 11-2f). This, too, is not surprising, for in this region both the marginal propensity to consume (and hence the multiplier) and the capital-output ratio (thus the accelerator effect) are large.

In the real world, where c is close to 1 and H considerably greater than 1, we are typically in region G, and thus the Samuelson model is not a model of the business cycle, but of explosive growth. It can be made to explain the cycle, however, wth some minor modifications proposed by Sir John Hicks (1904–).

III.   HICKS'S MODEL OF THE BUSINESS CYCLE

Hicks added two refinements: a full-employment ceiling, the level of which increases over time with growth in the labor force, and a

---

1. But not on the line $c = 1$. Remember $0 < c < 1$.

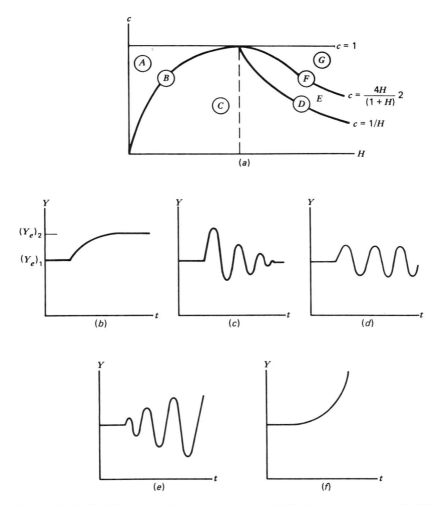

Figure 11-2. Multiplier accelerator model. *(a)* Critical values of *c* and *H*. *(b)* Decelerating growth. *(c)* Damped fluctuations. *(d)* Uniform fluctuations. *(e)* Explosive fluctuations. *(f)* Accelerating growth.

floor, based on the fact that there is always some autonomous investment being undertaken as new products are developed and new productive techniques discovered. Hicks assumes that the floor level, which is equal to the amount of autonomous investment multiplied by the investment multiplier, also increases over time. The floor and ceiling, depicted in Figure 11-3, form a channel within which the level of real output can fluctuate

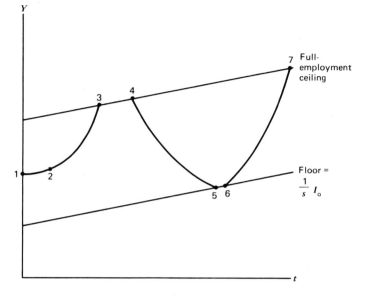

Figure 11-3. Hicks's theory of the cycle.

Suppose that the level of real output is growing steadily along a path such as 1–2 in Fig. 11-3. At 2 a slight increase in autonomous investment occurs, which, given the real-world values of c and H, leads to explosive growth (2–3 in the diagram). At point 3 real output comes up against the ceiling (3–4). Between points 3 and 4 the rate of growth is slower than it was between 2 and 3 and the output of the capital goods industry declines. With investment declining, the multiplier-accelerator mechanism moves into reverse and a decline in real output ensues (4–5), which is arrested when contact is made with the floor at 5. Growth in Y then occurs along the floor from 5 to 6. With Y increasing, the multipler-accelerator mechanism causes another takeoff along the explosive growth path (6–7), and at 7 the events described at 3 are repeated.

IV.   HARROD-DOMAR: THE EQUILIBRIUM GROWTH PATH

It sometimes happens that two researchers, following related but slightly different paths, reach virtually the same conclusion. The British economist Sir Roy Harrod (1900–   ), and Evsey Domar (1914–   ) an American, managed to do this, and ever since their names have been inextricably linked in the Harrod-Domar model of equilibrium growth.

The starting point is the capital-output ratio, defined in this instance in terms of the total output of goods and services, and not only consumer goods as it was in the Samuelson model.

$$h = \frac{K}{Y} \text{ the capital-output ratio.}$$

If K increases by an amount ΔK (=I), then aggregate supply increases by ΔY *where*

$$\Delta Y = \frac{\Delta K}{h} = \frac{I}{h}$$

The question that interested Harrod and Domar was whether, and under what conditions, an increase in output ΔY would generate sufficient aggregate demand to ensure that it would be purchased. If the increase in aggregate demand were insufficient, output would fall and unemployment increase; too large an increase would be inflationary. Aggregate demand is introduced by way of the investment multiplier.

$$\frac{\Delta Y}{\Delta I} = \frac{1}{s}$$

which may be written

$$\Delta Y = \frac{\Delta I}{s}$$

where s = marginal propensity to save. If the increase in aggregate supply is to be equal to the increase in aggregate demand it follows that

$$\frac{\Delta I}{I} = \frac{s}{h}$$

which, by cross-multiplication, becomes

The left-hand side of this expression is the rate of growth of investment.[2] The right-hand side is a constant, being the ratio of two constants, the marginal propensity to save and the capital-output

---

2. The percentage rate of growth is $100\Delta I/I$. Since this expression lacks the 100, it is necessary to express, for example, a 5 percent rate of growth as 0.05, and so on.

ratio. The conclusion, therefore, is that for equilibrium growth, investment must grow at a constant rate equal to the ratio s/h.

The Harrod-Domar model is a simplification of reality, as all models are, of course, but in it perhaps the search for simplicity has been carried too far. Note that nowhere in the model is mention made of the size of the labor force. This is equivalent to assuming that capital and labor are always combined in the same proportions—that no substitution can occur between them. In a world where capital and labor are substitutes, and the labor force itself is not growing at the same rate as the stock of capital, the value of the model for policymakers is minimal.

V.   SCHUMPETER AND THE ROLE OF THE ENTREPRENEUR

The theories discussed so far in this chapter have either been mechanical, in the sense that automatic forces were at work to keep the economy close to a subsistence-level equilibrium or to make it fluctuate, or been nonoperational—the equilibrium growth path was mapped according to assumptions that were too restrictive to make the model of much value. Those who believe that people are the masters of their fate will find these theories distasteful and they will love Joseph Schumpeter's (1883–1950) scenario, which seeks to explain both economic growth and the business cycle.

Schumpeter's heroes were entrepreneurs, people of wide-ranging ambition, who seek not only worldly wealth, but also to found a dynasty. The secret of success, Schumpeter believed, was to be an innovator, someone who markets a new product or develops a new method of producing an old one. It is necessary to make a distinction between an inventor and an innovator. They may be one and the same person—Edwin Land of Polaroid being a good example—but more often they are not. Inventors may die penniless, and Schumpeter had little time for them. The innovator who appropriates the inventor's ideas, whether by fair means or foul, is the person who prospers.

In order to achieve goals, entrepreneurs are willing to take enormous risks. They need not inherit great wealth. Indeed an important part of the Schumpeterian mechanisn is the method entrepreneurs use to finance their schemes—borrowing from banks.

The starting point in Fig. 11-4 is an economy in equilibrium with real output constant (1–2). At point 2 an entrepreneur, perhaps to finance the development of a new product, arranges a bank loan and builds new manufacturing facilities. Real output begins to increase. The bank loan leads to an increase in the money supply. The entre-

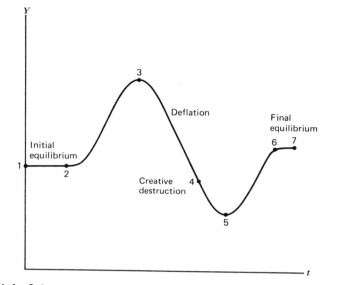

Figure 11-4. Schumpeter's mechanism for the business cycle and growth.

preneur bids up the price of resources to attract them from other sectors of the economy. As a result of both of these factors, the price level begins to rise.

Spurred by rising prices, a whole bevy of secondary entrepreneurs expand their output. These varied activities are represented in Fig. 11-4 by the move from 2 to 3.

At point 3 the first entrepreneur's new products are marketed. The revenues received are used to repay the bank loans, causing a decline in the money supply. With less money chasing more goods, deflation sets in, many of the secondary entrepreneurs who expanded their output in the expectation of receiving higher prices are disappointed, and a downturn in economic activity begins (3–4). As deflation progresses, less efficient operators are forced into bankruptcy, a process that Schumpeter called "creative destruction." He regarded this, not as a disaster, but as a necessary part of a Darwinian process that periodically weeds out the weak and the inefficient. As the economy become more efficient (point 5), an upswing in economic activity develops that carries real output to a new equilibrium (6–7), which is higher than the initial equilibrium at 1–2. Eventually this equilibrium is disturbed by the activities of another entrepreneur, and the cycle repeats itself over and over again.

Since each new equilibrium is higher than the previous one,

Schumpeter's model explains economic growth as well as the business cycle. In the United States one can point to the building of the railroads, the development of electric power, the introduction of the assembly line for the manufacture of automobiles, and, more recently, the multiplicity of applications of the transistor to television computers and communications as events that triggered a Schumpeterian cycle.

VI.   GOVERNMENT AS A SOURCE OF INSTABILITY AND GROWTH

Since World war II it has come to be accepted that government has a role to play in steering the economy between the Scylla of unemployment and the Charybdis of inflation and at the same time to head in the direction of a reasonable rate of economic growth. Given the proclivity of democratic governments to concentrate on one problem at a time, and to have a short time horizon that extends up to, but not beyond, the next election, government has itself become a source of instability, as Fig. 11-5 illustrates. With an election in the offing, the concern is to stimulate the economy so that unemployment is low, or at least declining, profits are healthy, and the country is bathed in an aura of prosperity that is conducive to the reelection of incumbent presidents, senators, and representatives.

Such policies tend to affect the level of output and employment first, the price level with a somewhat longer lag. If the timing is

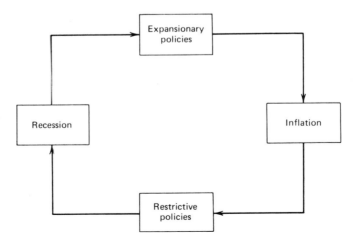

Figure 11-5. Government as a source of instability.

right, the inflation will not show up until after the election is safely decided. The first year or so of a new administration may then be devoted to slowing the rate of increase in prices, bringing on a recession about the middle of a president's four-year term. Concern then shifts to the next election and the monetary spigots are opened up once again and speeches are made about the need for tax cuts and increases in government spending in order to create more jobs. The cycle begins all over again.

The stock market, which parallels developments in the economy, has exhibited a tendency to follow a four-year cycle over the course of the last twenty years.

As was mentioned at the end of the previous chapter, appropriate government policies can stimulate economic growth. The United States is lagging behind its Western European and Japanese rivals in this regard, largely because the steps taken to stimulate the economy in times of recession have taken the form of cuts in the personal income tax, designed to stimulate consumption, and increases in government spending, particularly for the so-called job-creation programs of recent years. Increases in aggregate demand thus take the form of boosts in C and G, while I has been relatively neglected.

The Social Security system also has negative aspects. Believing that government will foot the bill in their old age, workers feel less compulsion to save. Funds are transferred from the working population to the elderly, who tend to have a higher marginal propensity to consume than do those in younger age brackets. Once again C is encouraged at the expense of S and I.

This is not to suggest that other countries do not have comparable arrangements to take care of the older segment of their population. They do. But usually the state-run pension funds invest their receipts in the private sector, promoting investment and growth. Many elected officials are already aware of the negative aspects of current economic policies. The need to stimulate investment and productivity is destined to be one of the more serious debates in the United States during the 1980s.

VII. SUMMARY AND CONCLUSION

Malthus took an extremely pessimistic view of economic prospects, believing that whenever output, the numerator of GNP per capita, rose, population, the denominator, also rose, ensuring that most humans were doomed to live out their days at, or close to, the subsistence level.

Samuelson developed a model based on the interaction of the

multiplier and the accelerator that could account for the business cycle, but that, in fact, given the real-world values of the key parameters, turned out to be a model of explosive growth.

Hicks, building on Samuelson's foundation by adding a full-employment ceiling and an autonomous-investment floor, succeeded in developing a convincing explanation for the business cycle.

Harrod and Domar investigated the conditions for stable economic growth, and Schumpeter accounted for both growth and the business cycle in a scenario that assigned the central role to the entrepreneur.

In recent years it appears that government itself, because of the fact that its policies take effect only after a lag, has become a source of instability. There are encouraging signs, however, that government now recognizes the need to stimulate investment and increase productivity.

QUESTIONS

1. Suppose that the capital-output ratio (K/C) is equal to 3.00. Which of the following marginal propensities to consume would result in: (1) explosive growth; (2) uniform fluctuations; (3) damped fluctuations; (4) explosive fluctuations?
   (a) $c = 0.60$.
   (b) $c = 0.25$.
   (c) $c = 0.85$.
   (d) $c = 0.33$.
2. Suppose that the marginal propensity to consume is 0.80 and the capital-output ratio (K/Y) is 1.60. At what percentage rate must investment grow for equilibrium growth?

12 | Other Post-Keynesian Developments

In the field of macroeconomics the name of John Maynard Keynes (1883–1946) is preeminent. Much of what you have read in the preceding chapters is a reflection of his thought, or that of other scholars building on the foundation he laid. All macroeconomists are Keynesians in the sense that the language of their field is the language of *The General Theory*. Yet the fact that people speak the same language does not mean that they necessarily agree with one another, and this statement is particularly true of macroeconomics. In this chapter we will examine some non-Keynesian viewpoints.

I. SOME ALTERNATIVE THEORIES OF THE CONSUMPTION FUNCTION

A major source of dissatisfaction with the Keynesian consumption function is its treatment of saving. In each year a certain proportion of income is saved. Over time the sum of these yearly savings represent an increase in wealth. In the language of Chapter 3, a flow variable (saving) eventually has an effect on a stock variable (wealth). Does not an increase in wealth affect consumption patterns, and hence saving? On this subject *The General Theory* is almost silent. The constancy of stock variables is ensured by the famous dictum that "in the long run we are all dead." Then why do people save? That question, too, does not receive a satisfactory answer. Other economists have sought the answer and their search has led them to new ideas about the nature of the consumption function.

A. Friedman: The Permanent-Income Hypothesis

$C = f(Y)$; consumption is a function of income. Here is the basis of all theories, but what time frame surrounds the basic picture? Is this week's consumption a function of this week's income? Or should we think in terms of months or years? Milton Friedman's (1912–) answer is that each individual has at least a rough idea of something called permanent income, the income the person expects to receive over a much longer time period than one year. Actual income on a monthly or yearly basis may differ slightly from permanent income because of such things as a lucky day at the races or an unexpected inheritance. In Friedman's terminology,

$$Y \quad = \quad Y_p \quad + \quad Y_t$$

Y	Y_p	Y_t
(Income)	(Permanent income)	(Transitory income)

Consumption may also be divided into a permanent component (C_p) and a transitory component (C_t), the former representing planned purchases, the latter the result of impulse buying.

The core of the permanent-income hypothesis is that

$$C_p = kY_p$$

This relationship differs from the Keynesian function in that there is no positive intercept on the C_p axis. k is a short-run constant. In the longer run it may vary slightly with changes in other economic variables, such as the rate of interest. Furthermore, and this is of crucial importance because of its policy implications, there is no relationship, other than a purely random one, between C_t and Y_t. An increase (or decrease) in transitory income does not lead to an increase (or decrease) in transitory consumption. Of four variables Y_p, Y_t, C_p, and C_t, there is only one line of causation, running from Y_p to C_p.

B. Duesenberry: The Relative-Income Hypothesis

James Duesenberry (1918–) also discards the notion of a positive intercept on the consumption axis.[1] Basically, consumption is directly proportional to income.

$$C = KY$$

---

1. J. S. Duesenberry, *Income, Savings, and the Theory of Consumer Behavior* (Harvard University Press, 1949).

But this is only an approximate relationship. Consumption is also affected by the level of income relative to the incomes of others with whom the consumer identifies. A doctor in a small city, for example, whose income is lower than that of most other doctors living there, consumes more than the basic relationship indicates. The doctor wants to do the same things and purchase the same products as other doctors. Keeping up with the Joneses is enshrined in economic theory. Conversely, a doctor with an income higher than that of most of his colleagues consumes less than indicated by the basic relationship. The relative-income hypothesis is so called because consumption depends not on income alone, but also on the level of that income relative to that of one's peers.

C. Ando, Brumberg, and Modigliani: The Life-Cycle Hypothesis

Associated with the names of Albert Ando,[2] Brumberg,[3] and Franco Modigliani, the life-cycle hypothesis posits that the relevant time frame for the consumption function is the longest possible period that an individual need consider: an entire lifetime. Lifetime consumption is equal to lifetime income, including inheritance, less the amount left to one's heirs. Or, rather, since lifetime income can only be guessed at, consumption depends on expected lifetime income.

The role of saving in this model is to smooth consumption patterns over time. A person's income typically follows the pattern shown in Fig. 12−1. When people start working, there is much to learn and employees are not as useful to an employer as they will be later when their skills are fully developed. Incomes reflect this fact, starting out relatively low at the beginning of a career (age 18 in Fig. 12−1), increasing over time, perhaps declining somewhat in later life as the aging process reduces productivity, but almost certainly declining precipitously when the age of retirement is reached (65 in Fig. 12−1, but undoubtedly higher in years to come as workers take advantage of recently enacted legislation setting the retirement age at 70).

Consumption follows a similar pattern without the extreme variations. In the early years, purchase of a home, furniture, and

---

2. A. Ando and F. Modigliani, "The Life-Cycle Hypothesis of Saving," *American Economic Review*, 53 (May 1963), pp. 55−84.

3. F. Modigliani and R. Brumberg, "Utility Analysis and the Consumption Function: An Interpretation of Cross-Section Data," in K. Kurihara, ed., *Post Keynesian Economics* (Rutgers University Press, 1954).

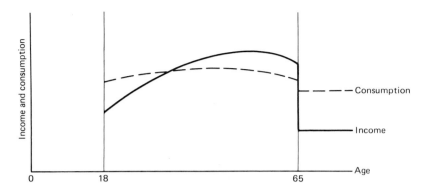

Figure 12-1. Life-cycle hypothesis.

appliances is financed by borrowing (negative saving). Later, at roughly age 35 in the diagram, consumption and income finally become equal. Then income exceeds consumption as debts are paid off. Eventually, when the mortgage is burned and other debts are reduced to zero, thoughts turn to additional saving to finance the retirement years. The more that can be saved in this period, the less consumption needs to drop when Social Security and perhaps a pension provide the only source of income.

The life-cycle hypothesis is an appealing one. It reflects the way most people appear to behave, and it supplies a clear rationale for saving that competing hypothesis lack.

D. Which Hypothesis is Valid?

With four hypotheses to choose from if we include the Keynesian absolute-income hypothesis discussed in Chapter 4, the question arises as to which best reflects the world of reality. Faced with such a question, economists turn to the econometrician for guidance. The absolute-income hypothesis predicts that there should be a positive intercept on the C-axis, while competing hypotheses suggest that the function starts at the origin.

In this instance the econometrician is not very helpful. To be sure, as was mentioned in Chapter 4, if a study is made of the consumption patterns of a number of families in a given year, the consumption function looks very much like Fig. 12−2*a* and lends support to the absolute-income hypothesis.

But we can also get a picture of the consumption function by plotting data on aggregate C and Y for a series of years; the plot looks much like Fig. 12−2*b*. Since the data for Fig. 12*a* all come from a single year, the function depicted there is often called the short-run consumption function, whereas Fig. 12–2b, based on data for a series of years, is called the long-run function. You can pick the theory you like and the econometrician can provide evidence in its favor. But then you have to explain away the evidence to the contrary.

E. Reconciling the Facts: The Absolute-Income Hypothesis

The short-run function provides evidence in favor of the absolute-income hypothesis. The task facing its proponents is therefore to explain away the long-run function. This they do very neatly by claiming that it is merely a statistical artifact. What appears to be a single function is really a series of points on a number of short-run functions that happen to be moving upward over time. In any given year the data supply only one point on the function, and while the complete series of points is consistent with Fig. 12–2b, it is also consistent with Fig. 12–3.

Why does the short-run function shift upward over time?

1. With increased life-expectancy, the population of the United States is growing older, and people of retirement age, whose income is lower than it once was, spend more of their incomes than their more youthful counterparts.
2. The migration from farm to factory continues unabated, and there are many more things to spend money on in the city than there are in the country.

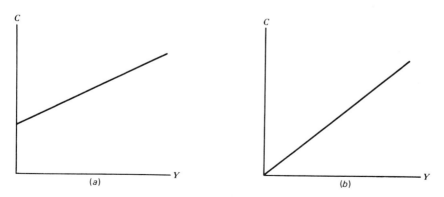

Figure 12-2. Two pieces of evidence. *(a)* Short-run consumption. *(b)* Long-run consumption.

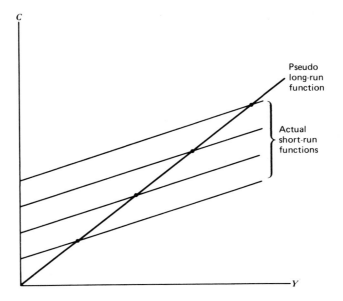

Figure 12-3. Absolute-income hypothesis—explaining away the long-run function.

3. Many items once regarded as luxuries—refrigerators, washing machines, and television sets, for example—are now considered necessities. Consumers no longer hesitate to purchase these big-ticket items, and readily go into debt to do so.
4. The nation's stock of wealth continues to increase. At some point in time wealth-holders decide that their nest egg is large enough, cut back their saving, and hence spend more.

F. Reconciling the Facts: The Relative-Income Hypothesis

Duesenberry finds the long-run consumption function consistent with his hypothesis. He explains the short-run function in terms of the business cycle (Fig. 12−4). As long as their income is increasing, consumers follow the long-run function (1−2 in the diagram). When a recession comes along and incomes decline, they resist a drop in their standard of living, and instead of moving back down the long-run function from 2 to 1, trace out a course from 2 to 3, depleting their savings to finance expenditures in excess of their income. In the ensuing upswing, their first thought is to replenish those savings and so they retrace the path from 3 to 2. At 2, with their savings

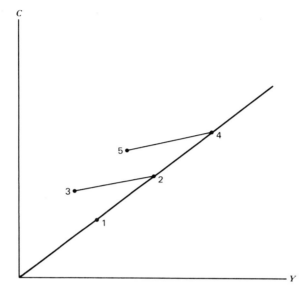

Figure 12-4. Relative-income hypothesis—explaining away the short-run function.

restored to a satisfactory level, they continue up the long-run function to 4, where, as another recession strikes, they move from 4 to 5 and back again as before. Points 2−3 and 4−5 appear to lie on two separate short-run functions. In fact, if you accept the relative-income hypothesis, they are merely deviations from the true, or long-run function, that forms the basis of the theory.

G. Reconciling the Facts: The Permanent-Income Hypothesis and the Life-Cycle Hypothesis

Since both the short-run and the long-run consumption function reflect a relationship between consumption and income with both measured on a yearly basis, neither Friedman nor Ando, Brumberg, and Modigliani can use either function as evidence in support of their hypotheses, but neither do they have to explain either of them away. Furthermore, since each hypothesis is based on expected levels of (permanent or lifetime) incomes, which of necessity cannot be measured, a statistical test of either is rather difficult. Friedman did develop a method for estimating permanent income and consumption, and did indeed find a proportional relationship between them, but the appeal of the life-cycle hypothesis rests on a knowledge of human behavior, rather than on any meaningful statistical evidence.

H. Policy Implications

The hypotheses we have just discussed are more than interesting theoretical constructs. They have important implications for the conduct of fiscal policy. Consider a temporary tax increase, designed to cool off a too rapid rate of inflation. If the absolute-income hypothesis is valid, the tax increase will reduce disposable income, consumption, and aggregate demand, just as Chapter 6 described.

But what if Duesenberry is right? A temporary tax increase reduces takehome pay, but since consumers resist a decline in their standard of living, consumption will not be cut back so much, and to that extent the tax increase is less effective in reducing aggregate demand.

The same is true if Friedman is correct. By definition, a temporary tax increase does not affect permanent income. Permanent consumption does not change, and since transitory consumption is unaffected by a change in transitory income, fiscal policy in this instance is ineffective. The same argument applies in reverse to the effect of a temporary tax cut, designed to reduce unemployment.

During Lyndon Johnson's presidency, a temporary tax surcharge was enacted in the hope of reducing a rising inflation rate. It was known to be temporary—one of Nixon's oft-voiced campaign promises was to rescind it, and Nixon was the clear frontrunner in the 1968 presidential race. In the face of that tax increase inflation continued unabated and in fact worsened. Should we assume that temporary tax surcharges are ineffective and thus reject the absolute-income hypothesis, a major bulwark of Keynesian analysis? Certainly the non-Keynesian schools of thought have grown in stature since that episode, but it cannot be considered conclusive. The waters were muddied by the fact that the Federal Reserve offset the effects of the tax surcharge by means of an easy-money policy. The Johnson tax surcharge was not, therefore, just a test of the absolute-income hypothesis versus the permanent- or relative-income hypotheses; it also represented a test of strength between fiscal and monetary policy. But whatever the reason for the outcome, it represented a blow to one of the bastions of Keynesian orthodoxy.

II.   MONETARISTS AND MONETARISM

Within thirty years of the publication of *The General Theory*, Keynesian doctrine had gained almost universal acceptance throughout the Western world. The use of the word *almost* is necessary because in the United States two outposts of an alternative economic philosophy held out undismayed by the success of the invader from across the Atlantic. The University of Chicago and the Federal Reserve Bank of St. Louis remained true to monetarism. In the last ten years they have led, with no little success, the monetarist counterattack against Keynesian dogma.

Monetarists believe that the most important determinant of the level of economic activity is the money supply. Ask monetarists what caused the Great Depression of the 1930s and they will reply, a decline in the stock of money as runs on banks extinguished billions of dollars in demand deposits. Ask them what lies behind the inflation of the 1970s and the response will be a too rapid rate of growth in the money supply. M_1 (currency plus demand deposits) grew from $219.7 billion in 1970 to $338.5 billion in 1977, a compounded annual rate of growth of 6.4 percent per year, which closely parallels the 6.6 percent rate of increase in the consumer price index over the same time period.[4]

As with most movements, its practitioners run the gamut from moderate to extreme. An extreme monetarist would argue that fiscal policy is completely ineffective since deficit spending only affects the level of economic activity to the extent that the deficit is financed by an increase in the money supply—monetary policy in disguise. If the deficit is financed by government borrowing, the argument continues, the sale of government bonds depresses bond prices, raises interest rates, and "crowds out" an amount of private investment that exactly offsets the increase in aggregate demand caused by an increase in government spending, or an increase in consumption resulting from a cut in taxes. A more moderate monetarist would hold that "crowding out" is not complete—that only some of the increase in aggregate demand is offset.

To say that fiscal policy is ineffective is to say that the V of $MV = PQ$ stays relatively constant, at least in the short run. Monetarists do not believe in the existence of a speculative demand for money. This means, as Fig. 12−5 illustrates, that the money-demand function, consisting only of a transactions demand, is a vertical line.[5] If we now add to that diagram a money-supply function, there appears to be no equilibrium where $L = M$. In the monetarist scheme of things, equilibrium is brought about, not by changes in the interest

4. Source: *Economic Report of the President,* 1979, pp. 239 and 251.

5. Most monetarists would not deny that, at very high interest rates, the transactions-demand function bends backwards as large institutions and corporations make do with smaller transactions balances, reflecting the opportunity cost of holding them.

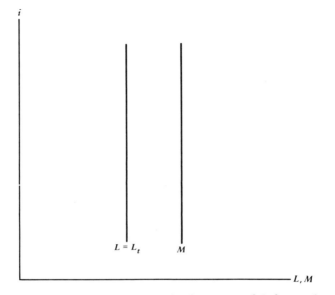

Figure 12-5. Money supply and demand—the monetarist viewpont.

rate, but by changes in the price level. With the supply of money exceeding the demand, holders of excess money balances get rid of them by exchanging money for goods, increasing the demand for goods and bidding up their price.[6] At higher levels of P, and hence of $Y (=PQ)$, L_t increases until it is equal to M, when the process comes to a halt.

Given the importance monetarists attach to the role of money, one would assume that monetarists would advocate the active use of monetary policy to control the level of economic activity. Nothing could be further from the truth.

Monetarists believe that when the Federal Reserve pursues an active policy in an effort to stabilize the ups and downs of the business cycle it actually makes things worse. This is because the effects of monetary policy are felt only with a lag that is both long and variable. It takes time before one can be certain as to exactly what phase of the business cycle we are in. Shortly after he took office in 1974, President Gerald R. Ford was handing out WIN

---

6. If some resources are unemployed, the output of goods may increase also. Either way Y increases.

(standing for Whip Inflation Now) buttons. Within a matter of months he was desperately attempting to cope with the worst recession in the United States since World War II.

Even when policymakers know exactly what the problem is, and have taken the necessary action, their response does not affect the level of economic activity immediately. An increase in the money supply, for example, causes an increase in real output some six months or more later, and affects the price level after an even longer period of time.

In Fig. 12−6, a recession beginning in month 6 may not be apparent until month 9, and easy-money policies adopted then may just be beginning to affect the price level in month 20, when the recession is already over, and incipient inflation is the problem of more immediate concern. Such misguided actions, monetarists argue, are destabilizing and make the swings in economic activity wider than they would otherwise be.

What should be the goal of monetary policy? Monetarists believe that it should be to allow the money supply to grow at a constant rate, equal to the rate of growth in real output. If this policy is pursued consistently, they argue, the economy will eventually settle down in a pattern of steady growth with a stable price level.

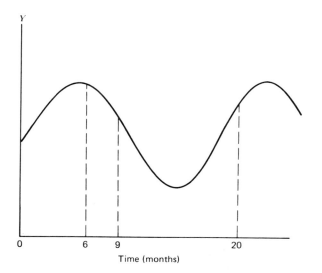

Figure 12-6. Why not to pursue an active monetary policy—the monetarist viewpoint.

III. RATIONAL EXPECTATIONS

The school of rational expectations has its headquarters in the state of Minnesota, at the University of Minnesota and the Federal Reserve Bank of Minneapolis. Its major tenets are that people are rational, pursue their own self-interest in the best tradition of *The Wealth of Nations,* and foresee the effects of a policy change as soon as it is implemented.

A cut in taxes designed to lower the rate of unemployment, for example, causes business firms to raise their prices and labor unions to demand higher wages, because of the eventual inflation that both foresee resulting from the stimulative fiscal policy. Instead of the tax cut increasing output and reducing unemployment, therefore, its only effect is to kick up the rate of inflation.

The policy implication of a belief in the theory of rational expectations is much the same as follows from the espousal of monetarism: fiscal and monetary policy should follow a steady-as-you-go course, enabling private-sector decisionmakers to make long-range plans with little fear that unpleasant economic surprises will make them go awry.

IV. THE LAFFER CURVE AND THE WEDGE

Ever since the publication of *The General Theory,* the accent in macroeconomics has been on aggregate demand. Aggregate supply was assumed fixed in the short run, and in the long run we are all dead. In recent times, Arthur Laffer, a Californian economist, has questioned that assumption and suggested that macroeconomists ought to focus their attention on ways to increase aggregate supply.

The centerpiece of Laffer's approach is the "Laffer Curve," depicting a relationship between tax rates and tax revenues. His starting point is to note that tax revenues will be equal to zero at two rates of taxation: 0 and 100 percent. If the tax rate is 0 percent, revenues will obviously be equal to zero, while at a 100 percent rate, meaning that the whole of a person's income goes to the government, there is no incentive to work and so both income and tax revenues will be zero (Fig. 12–7).

Any other level of tax revenue, up to, but not including, the maximum of $310 billion, may be obtained by either one of two tax rates. A tax revenue of $220 billion, for example, could be collected either with a tax rate of 10 percent (point *a* in the diagram), or with a tax rate of 68 percent (point *b*). At *a,* what Laffer calls the "wedge," the difference between what a person earns and the takehome pay is small. Everyone has an incentive to work hard, to undertake risky

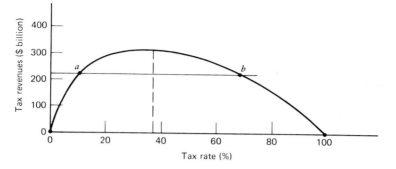

Figure 12-7. Laffer curve.

ventures, and to seek out further sources of income, because they get to keep 90 percent of everything they make. At *b*, by contrast, the wedge is much larger. With government taking 68 percent of gross income, the incentive to exert oneself in order to increase one's income is much less. Absenteeism becomes chronic among the labor force, and entrepreneurs limit their activities to fairly risk-less pursuits. Tax revenues at *a* and *b* are equal, but at *a* government is taking a small percentage of a large national income and at *b* a large percentage of a much smaller national income. The maximum possible tax revenue of $310 billion can be obtained at only one tax rate—37 percent in the diagram.

Now we come to the crucial point in the Laffer argument. If tax rates are higher than 37 percent, a cut in tax rates will not only expand aggregate supply and national income by increasing incentives, but will also increase tax revenues. Here is indeed a case where we can have our cake and eat it too. At one stroke the rate of inflation, the rate of unemployment, and the budget deficit are all reduced. Inflation slows because the *Q* of *MV = PQ* increases. With *M* and *V* constant, *P* must decline. Unemployment falls because workers have a stronger incentive to seek jobs, and employers need those workers in order to expand output. Tax revenues increase and reduce the budget deficit. It does appear that there is a free lunch after all. Indeed, there may be, but first we must stop and think what we really know about the Laffer curve.

The rationale on which it is based is certainly plausible. High tax rates do stifle initiative. Very high tax rates may even drive particu-larly gifted individuals to emigrate (Ingmar Bergman, the movie di-rector, left his native Sweden for that reason). Yet the only two points on the curve of which we can be certain are the two extreme points on the tax-rate axis—0 and 100 percent. All other points that lie in between are purely conjectural. Would we get the same tax revenues from tax rates of 10 and 68 percent? We do not know. Do we get maximum tax revenues with a tax rate of 37 percent? We do not know. We do not even know—and this is the flaw in Laffer's argument—whether or not we are to the right or to the left of the high point on the curve. Those members of Congress, mostly members of the Republican Party, who believe that we are to the right, support the Kemp-Roth bill, which would cut taxes by 30 percent over a three-year period. Those who feel that we are to the left, a majority when these lines were written in early 1980, believe that a tax cut, through stimulating aggregate demand, would be inflationary and oppose it. Which of these two viewpoints is the right one?

Certainly the burden of taxation on the average American has increased by leaps and bounds over the past ten years as inflation has pushed taxpayers into ever higher tax brackets. Productivity is certainly declining, in large part due to the disincentives that exist today. But passage of the Kemp-Roth bill would be a calculated risk. We would not find where we are on the Laffer curve until after its enactment.

V.   THE FUTURE OF MACROECONOMICS

Keynes once said that practical people are all the slaves of some defunct economist. It would be the supreme irony if, during the 1980s, Keynes turned out to be the defunct economist of whom the politicians in Washington were the slaves, at a time when macroeconomics has advanced well beyond the ground covered by *The General Theory.*

Yet in fairness to Keynes we need to remind ourselves that deficit spending is a specific remedy for a specific disease: widespread unemployment brought on by a deficiency in aggregate demand. Policymakers who call themselves Keynesians when they run horrendous budget deficits during periods of inflation take his name in vain. Deficits caused by a lack of will to balance a budget through fear of the political consequences of increasing taxes, or cutting spending, have nothing to do with Keynesian economics—or any other brand of economics, for that matter.

If the problem of cost-push inflation that plagued the United States for most of the 1970s served to break down the boundaries, which in any event were of an artificial nature, between macroeconomics and microeconomics, that will be all to the good. The solution to cost-push inflation is to be found in making labor markets more competitive, a microeconomic problem, although, given the political power of the labor movement, it is even more a political problem.

What advice should the macroeconomist give the politician or administrator who genuinely wants to see the American economy restored to its old track of low unemployment, low inflation, and steady economic growth? Are we to seek solutions from the Keynesians, the Monetarists, or the school of rational expectations, or is the Laffer curve to be our guide for the future?

A good adviser is willing to accept solutions from any source, and the difference between the various viewpoints is not so great as to make every policy question an either/or proposition. Consider the difference between the Keynesians and the followers of Laffer. The former suggest that a tax cut, or an increase in spending, is the remedy for a recession. The latter propose a cut in tax rates as a means of reducing inflation, unemployment, and the size of the budget deficit. A compromise may be reached very easily. When a recession comes along, cut taxes. As the economy rebounds, Keynesians can point to the effect of an increase in aggregate demand, the Lafferites to the beneficial effects on aggregate supply. There will doubtless be a modicum of truth in both viewpoints, but the important consideration is that in certain circumstances an agreed solution is available.

Many Keynesians do not agree with the monetarist prescription of permitting the money supply to grow at a uniform rate. They, and perhaps a majority of politicians, prefer to pursue a more active policy. Again, a compromise is at hand: make changes in the policy variables when it is felt that the need arises, but do so at fairly long intervals. There is no need for the Federal Reserve to intervene in the bond markets three or four times a day in the course of conducting open-market operations. The only beneficiaries of such a policy are the bond brokers, whose commissions are swollen by the Fed's activities.

Wide swings in monetary policy, as when M_2 grew at an annual rate of 2.7 percent from October 1978 to March 1979, and then skyrocketed at an annual rate of 11.5 percent between March and June 1979, are quite unnecessary. Changes in the rate of growth of one or two percentage points are all that are needed to pursue an active policy. The differences between activist Keynesians and passive monetarists can be narrowed even if not eliminated.

What can be foreseen as macroeconomics approaches its golden jubilee? The name of Keynes will still be revered, although the emphasis will shift from concern with aggregate demand to aggregate supply. Economists should avoid making predictions as they would a swarm of angry bees, but this one is willing to forecast that the competition between the varied macroeconomic schools of thought will not result in a clear-cut victory for any one, but that a synthesis of the better ideas of all of them will become the accepted macroeconomics of the future.

VI. SUMMARY AND CONCLUSION

Economists have developed alternatives to the Keynesian consumption function: (1) Friedman's permanent-income hypothesis; (2) Duesenberry's relative-income hypothesis; and (3) the life-cycle hypothesis, associated with the names of Ando, Brumberg, and Modigliani.

The empirical evidence does not provide clear-cut support for any one of these competing hypotheses, yet choosing between them is important because of their implications for policymaking.

Monetarists emphasize the importance of money in economic affairs, but believe that the pursuit of an activist monetary policy is destabilizing. They recommend instead that the money supply be permitted to grow at a constant rate roughly equal to the rate of growth of real output.

Followers of the school of national expectations agree that both fiscal and monetary policy should not be subject to abrupt changes, while the followers of Arthur Laffer emphasize the role of tax cuts in stimulating productivity and investment.

The author believes that the new macroeconomics will be synthesis of the better ideas of several schools of thought. Whether or not he is correct, only time will tell.

QUESTIONS

1. (a) What is the major source of dissatisfaction with the Keynesian consumption function?
   (b) What is the only causal relationship in the permanent-income hypothesis?
   (c) If you are living beyond your means in order to keep up with a group of friends who are almost all richer than you are, you best exemplify which theory of the consumption function?
   (d) What does an extreme monetarist have to say about the efficacy of fiscal policy? Why?
2. Outline four reasons that a true believer in the absolute-income hypothesis might give to account for the short-run consumption function shifting upward over time.

3. Name the school of economic thought that might be expected to approve of the following policy prescriptions:
   (a) The Federal Reserve should let the money supply grow at a constant rate, roughly equal to the rate of growth of real output.
   (b) Cut taxes to fight inflation.
   (c) Both fiscal and monetary policy should follow a "steady-as-you-go" course.
   (d) A temporary tax surcharge will be effective in reducing the rate of inflation.

Index